Cla

Key Concepts series

Barbara Adam, *Time*
Alan Aldridge, *Consumption*
Alan Aldridge, *The Market*
Jakob Arnoldi, *Risk*
Will Atkinson, *Class*
Colin Barnes and Geof Mercer, *Disability*
Darin Barney, *The Network Society*
Mildred Blaxter, *Health 2nd edition*
Harriet Bradley, *Gender 2nd edition*
Harry Brighouse, *Justice*
Mónica Brito Vieira and David Runciman, *Representation*
Steve Bruce, *Fundamentalism 2nd edition*
Joan Busfield, *Mental Illness*
Margaret Canovan, *The People*
Andrew Jason Cohen, *Toleration*
Alejandro Colás, *Empire*
Mary Daly, *Welfare*
Anthony Elliott, *Concepts of the Self 3rd edition*
Steve Fenton, *Ethnicity 2nd edition*
Katrin Flikschuh, *Freedom*
Michael Freeman, *Human Rights 2nd edition*
Russell Hardin, *Trust*
Geoffrey Ingham, *Capitalism*
Fred Inglis, *Culture*
Robert H. Jackson, *Sovereignty*
Jennifer Jackson Preece, *Minority Rights*
Gill Jones, *Youth*
Paul Kelly, *Liberalism*
Anne Mette Kjær, *Governance*
Ruth Lister, *Poverty*
Jon Mandle, *Global Justice*
Cillian McBride, *Recognition*
Anthony Payne and Nicola Phillips, *Development*
Judith Phillips, *Care*
Chris Phillipson, *Ageing*
Michael Saward, *Democracy*
John Scott, *Power*
Timothy J. Sinclair, *Global Governance*
Anthony D. Smith, *Nationalism 2nd edition*
Deborah Stevenson, *The City*
Leslie Paul Thiele, *Sustainability*
Steven Peter Vallas, *Work*
Stuart White, *Equality*
Michael Wyness, *Childhood*

Class

Will Atkinson

polity

Copyright © Will Atkinson 2015

The right of Will Atkinson to be identified as Author of this Work has been asserted in accordance with the UK Copyright, Designs and Patents Act 1988.

First published in 2015 by Polity Press

Polity Press
65 Bridge Street
Cambridge CB2 1UR, UK

Polity Press
350 Main Street
Malden, MA 02148, USA

ISBN-13: 978-0-7456-8512-0
ISBN-13: 978-0-7456-8513-7(pb)

A catalogue record for this book is available from the British Library.

Library of Congress Cataloging-in-Publication Data

Atkinson, Will, 1983-
    Class / Will Atkinson.
        pages cm. – (Key concepts series)
    Includes bibliographical references and index.
    ISBN 978-0-7456-8512-0 (hardback : alk. paper) – ISBN 978-0-7456-8513-7 (pbk. : alk. paper)   1. Social classes.   2. Social conflict.   I. Title.
    HT609.A8498 2015
    305.5–dc23
                            2015000759

Typeset in 10.5 on 12 pt Sabon
by Toppan Best-set Premedia Limited
Printed and bound in the UK by CPI Group (UK) Ltd, Croydon, CRO 4YY

For further information on Polity, visit our website: politybooks.com

Contents

1
Introduction

The sheer variety of things the concept of 'class' appears to cover can sometimes seem bewildering, if not downright contradictory, to those who want to get a handle on it. Everyday conversations, news stories and opinion pieces, but academic research too, all buzz with loose and vague uses which, on closer inspection, might not be all that easy to reconcile. Sometimes, for example, it is used to capture the recently popular notion of a divide between the bankers, or the 1 per cent in income terms, and the 99 per cent of us. At other times it is deployed to make sense of cruel exploitation in dingy workshops around the globe, or tension and conflict between managers and workers in workplaces across the world, or governments being run by people coming from a small number of elite educational institutions thanks to extremely wealthy – even aristocratic – backgrounds. Then again it seems linked to abject poverty, exclusion and deprivation, or is touted as a cause of lack of social mobility or early death.

At the same time, class is often held to account in some way for rather more pervasive and seemingly ordinary things such as the clothes we wear, the food we eat, the music we listen to, the houses we live in, the way we walk and talk, our plans and aspirations, our dreams and our hopes, our skills and our knowledge, our interests, our morals and our politics. It seems to be simply there in everything we do, what we can do, what we want to do and our relationship with others, so that when we see others we instantly read their place in the world relative to ours through what they are wearing, what they are saying, how they are saying it or what they are doing. We feel we have something in common or not, that we are more or less like each other, and we look up to them or, more perniciously, we look down on them. When we talk of (or to) them, furthermore, we mobilize a vast vocabulary sharpened for the task of distinguishing, differentiating and denigrating, that is, doing down, criticizing, judging the worth of a person in relation to ourselves – words such as 'snob', 'toff', 'commoner', 'scumbag', but also 'classy', 'smart', 'sophisticated', 'stupid', 'vulgar', 'tasteless', 'dangerous', 'unfortunate' and so on. And of course not everyone possesses equal capacity, equal power, to make their definitions of people stick, to spread them widely and impose them as legitimate, or to deflect or cushion damaging blows to self-worth dispensed by others.

So how can one concept seem to cover so much? How can it account for all of these things at the same time? Are some of the things mentioned really about class, or are they just signs of confusion which needs to be cleared up? Certainly social scientists have to be wary of the multiple, conflicting, fuzzy and confused definitions of 'class' circulating in the media, politics and everyday conversation. We have to break with those folk constructs, those 'prenotions' as Emile Durkheim called them, and put them to one side since part of our interest is in understanding where they come from and what interests they might serve. Yet social science is just as plagued by competing definitions purporting to be able to explain different things – or, to be more accurate, to explain lots of things in very different ways – usually deriving from clashing ideas about what it means to be human.

The primary aim of this book, then, is to clarify matters for those new to the topic of class. Inevitably there will be some taking stock of where we are currently at, assessment of which directions seem to offer the most fruitful ways forward, taking stances in particular debates and developing possible avenues for further work. Nevertheless, the first and foremost task is to offer an accessible guide to the concept of class, and to achieve this it sets out to explore five sets of relevant questions and the answers given by different schools of thought. The first of these questions, and the most fundamental, is this: what actually *is* social class? Is it defined by economic situation, education, occupation, some combination, or what? Are there clear boundaries between classes, so that we can separate out categories and say who is in one and who is in another on the basis of some criteria? If so, how many classes are there, and what labels should we use for them? Or is there just one continuous hierarchy from top to bottom that cannot meaningfully be cut up at any point? Or multiple hierarchies which combine to give individuals multifaceted positions?

Second, how do sociologists *study* social class? How do we 'operationalize' it, or, more simply, how do we convert a theoretical concept into a tool of research (which is, of course, what it should be)? Is it best mobilized as a variable in large-scale statistical research looking at national patterns or treated as an element of experience in in-depth qualitative research – or can we use it to pursue both, and if so, how?

Third, what is its relationship with *other* forms of social division such as gender and ethnicity? Given increased migration, the rise of multicultural politics and the fact that women are more represented in the upper echelons of the education system and the workforce than ever, how exactly do these alternative divisions offset or reinforce class? Have they increased in potency, maybe eclipsing class, or are they subordinate to class, or compounded by class? Does the concept of class adequately make space for other divisions or does its blindness to them make it useless?

Leading on from this, could it be that social changes in the last century have made class less *relevant* today? Does it apply only to the past, as a useful way of interpreting history? As we will see, there are plenty of people, academics and non-academics, who have argued that the sun has now set on the concept of class. More people than ever before go to university nowadays, they declare, hardly anyone works in factories or things such as mining any more in the Western world (and in the Far East the concept of class is supposedly irrelevant), everyone dresses with individual style in contemporary consumer societies, and political parties in wealthy nations have become so similar they can hardly be said to represent warring class interests.

Finally, and grounding the answer to the last question, what are the observable *effects* of social class on people's lives, and how exactly does it produce them? Given what we know about the different definitions of class, what is the causal relationship between social class and certain patterns in educational outcomes, health, political allegiances or lifestyle choices, and which outcomes should we consider to be the most important in the grand scheme of things? As will soon become apparent, this varies considerably according to the theory of class you subscribe to.

These, then, are the five clusters of questions the book seeks to answer. There is, however, one rather basic set of questions which should be answered before any other: where exactly did this concept of 'class' come from in the first place? When was it first used, what did it refer to then, how did it evolve over time, and how did it relate to the varying social structures of different historical eras? These are important questions not least for clarifying that the notion of 'class' is much older than capitalism and the familiar language of 'upper', 'middle' and 'working class' that came with it, even if it is, admittedly, in capitalist societies that the most rigorous and vigorous attention has been given to it.

A brief history of 'class'

Let us start right at the beginning, with the birth of the word 'class' itself. It derives from the Latin *classis*, first coined in the sixth century BC during the administration of the Roman King Servius Tullius – long before Rome was an Empire or even a Republic. Literally meaning 'a summoning', it served the eminently functional purpose of helping the rulers of the day categorize the population so as to determine their voting rights. This was based on a simple classification of loose social standing as given by age, amount of land possessed and number of men one could call to arms if necessary (Calvert, 1982). No rigorous criteria were used beyond that, it involved no conception of relations between the different classifications (of dependence or antagonism, for example), and it had no real impact on people's perception of the world, which was still at the time structured around tribal ancestry and honour. Yet the notion was born and lingered in the ether.

Only when the ancient Greeks, among them Plato and Aristotle, came along a bit later did the divisions and relations between categorizations and hierarchical rankings of types of people – slaves and citizens, peasants and nobles and so on – become an issue of intellectual discussion and significance demanding analytical energy. So we have Plato setting out the ideal hierarchy for the smooth running of city-states such as Athens in his most celebrated work, *The Republic*, with the philosopher-king at the top and its various ranks of trained guardians, and Aristotle ruminating about the antagonistic relations between the rich, the poor and those in between in his writings on political philosophy. Despite the impression given by most translations, however, no Greek equivalent of the term 'class' was actually used to analyse any of this – they tended to use vaguer terms such as 'groups' and 'categories' instead, or more specific terms denoting honour, ethnicity, tribe or social role. In fact, after a long period of being confined to its strict Latin connotation, the notion of 'class' as a specific description of social relations only really wormed its way into the English language in the seventeenth century AD. At that time, England was still, like most of the Western world, in the process of shaking off its feudal past, which had dominated social relations from just after the fall of the Roman Empire, and so this new-fangled term had to contend with the labels used to make sense of the perceived rankings of superiority and inferiority generated in that system, such as 'social rank', 'grade', 'position', 'standing', 'station', 'estate' and so on (Williams, 2001).

In feudal societies a monarch possessed all the land within a certain territory. He or she, however, parcelled it out to nobles such as barons, as well as bishops, in return for loyalty and favours such as money, soldiers or administrative functions; the nobles in turn parcelled it out to knights (generally called vassals), again in return for loyalty and favours; and the knights in turn had the peasantry – the vast majority of the population – work on their land for their keep. Though the constant internecine wars and struggles between the nobility of the Middle Ages, so clearly documented by Elias (2000), make it all too clear that this system was far from stable and uncontested, positions in the feudal order were mostly hereditary. Moreover, these were the so-called 'Dark Ages' in Western Europe, where open-minded thought on social relations had been washed away with the fall of the Roman Empire and Christianity monopolized what intellectual activity there was. As a result, the feudal power structure was generally believed to be divinely ordained, that is to say, in accordance with the will of God. It was also believed, for this very reason, that such a hierarchy must be fully functional and necessary for a harmonious society. It was probably not so harmonious for the peasants, eking a living out of the land, but it was certainly not to be transgressed in case that made one ungodly and, so far as they were concerned, likely to be frazzled in the furnaces of hell. Unsurprisingly, therefore, people tended not to question their station in life – if you were born a poor peasant it was because God wanted you to be one, so fulfil your functions as best you can and defer to those God has chosen to be superior to you and you may just be rewarded in the afterlife. Certainly this was the vision supported by those at the top of the supposed 'divine chain of being'.

There had always been pockets of resistance to this, especially in times of famine, but by the eighteenth century feudalism and its religious justifications had finally crumbled away. The Enlightenment was upon us, and thinkers such as Jean-Jacques Rousseau and the French *philosophes* (Diderot, Voltaire, Montesquieu) as well as Thomas Paine (in *The Rights of Man*) began to question tradition, mysticism and superstition and to favour reason over blind faith. Social structures and inequalities were therefore no longer seen as ordained by God but as a human product, created by humans through the course of history. There emerged a belief that all humans are essentially born equal, made of the same stuff, with nothing intrinsically tying us to any role or station in life, and so inequality no longer seemed necessarily fair and functional but arbitrary, unjust and in need of change. Rousseau's famous phrase was 'man [and woman, we would add] is born free' – that is, born *equal*, born the same – 'and everywhere he [and she] is in chains' – i.e. in the shackles of social organization.

The Enlightenment did not come from nowhere, of course, but was facilitated by the growing prosperity and urbanization of the time, since this allowed certain people enough freedom from the pressures of feeding and clothing themselves to be able to question the world and think for a living. The emergence and growth of the university system across Europe and its detachment from the church also made a difference. However, this prosperity, urbanization and educational development were themselves rooted in long-running shifts in the nature of power and domination that had been going on since at least the sixteenth century – some say earlier. The precise nature and pace of events in each nation were different and the general underlying causes are still hotly debated, but the overarching theme was a growing competition between the honour and loyalty sustaining the feudal system on the one hand and the rising power of money on the other. While this is often thought of as primarily a European-born phenomenon, moreover, in reality the struggle was deeply entangled with and spilt over into the violent acquisition, plunder and settlement of colonies – including the United States, where a quasi-feudal South vied with the money-oriented North-East until the Civil War (Mann, 1986).

In a nutshell, peasants and lords had begun to trade and sell their surpluses, to buy in labour rather than work themselves and to purchase, sell and enclose land – all of these had become commodities with an exchangeable economic price (see Polanyi, 1957). The intergenerational pathways through this steady transition were of several types: some lords turned their lands into profit-making ventures, some poorer peasants were kicked off their land and forced to find paid work in urban areas, some lords and wealthier peasants began to specialize in trade and, eventually, bring together landless workers into a factory production system – all spurred by and spurring the concurrent Industrial Revolution. No longer able to produce for themselves, these workers had to rely on their wages to purchase the things they needed to survive, extending and deepening national commodity markets for which proliferating factories increasingly produced. As the factory system grew through the seventeenth to nineteenth centuries, a mushrooming demand for specialized employees capable of overseeing workers, machines and processes saw the emergence of a range of specialists relying on technical or intellectual capacities. Likewise, the shift from feudal monarchy to bureaucratic, democratic nation states – with all its different timings and trajectories in different nations – was entwined with the appearance of a state elite relying on a specific education and training rather than lineage or honour to legitimize their power to rule (Weber, 1978; Bourdieu, 2004a).

This, then, was the steady process of change from feudalism to capitalism, and the struggle between noble and peasant slipped off the historical stage in the West. The main source of social and political conflicts and struggles was now perceived by many to be that between the new mass of urban factory workers and those who owned the factories, employed the workers and made money off the goods they produced. At the dawn of capitalism, a group of French economists called the Physiocrats had already begun to use the label 'class' (or the French equivalent, *classe*) to denote positions in the production process rather than simply social standing, and so, following their lead, many people, but most consistently and influentially one Karl Marx (1818–83), started labelling these two categories – workers and owners – 'classes'. So we had the 'labouring classes', or the 'working class' or 'proletariat', versus the 'capitalist class' or the 'bourgeoisie'. This does not mean, however, that this was the correct or even the only view of 'class' around: many wanted to use the label simply to capture the fact that social position was now made or attained rather than given by birth, and they saw the production process per se as less fundamental than the divisions between certain occupations or differences of skill, education or lifestyle. On these criteria people often, as David Cannadine (1998) has explored, identified three classes – lower, middle and upper – but sometimes more, and saw the distinctions and conflicts between these as more important.

This was true of politicians and social commentators, but it was also increasingly true of academic sociology, which had established itself in universities in Europe and America by the beginning of the twentieth century and concerned itself with the new divisions created by capitalism. From Max Weber (1864–1920) onwards, a driving focus was the rigorous conceptualization of classes for the purpose of describing and explaining their effects on people's lives, on political struggles and, given that capitalism was supposed to allow more freedom than feudalism, on social mobility. This was often done *against* Marxism, which was rising in prominence across the world due to the Russian revolution in 1917 and then, after the Second World War, with the spread of communism to other countries and the onset of the Cold War. It was only later in the century that Marxism managed to gain a respectable foothold in Western sociology, remaining until then a marginal force in the academy, but it is testimony to its worldwide significance as a political ideology that the understanding of class put forward by Marx had and still has a strong grip on political and popular discourse on the topic. Many people through the twentieth century associated class with trade unions and their battles with big business owners or managers (or nowadays with bankers and fat cats living off 'the 99 per cent'), even if this jostled with competing understandings of class around, such as the common three-tier model of lower, middle and upper, with their particular lifestyles and associated terms such as 'our betters', 'high society', 'middle England/America' and so on.

The fall and rise of 'class'

So what about the concept of class today? Has it stood the test of time? Of course the vast majority of the world can still be described as capitalist in one way or another, but it looks very different from the nascent system investigated by Marx and Weber a hundred-odd years ago. Since the Second World War in particular there have been swift and substantial changes in the Western world – enough to make some question whether 'class' as conceived by the thinkers of yesteryear really does any useful sociological work any more. Three of these changes are particularly important: the onset of post-industrialism, the rise of neoliberalism and the emergence of new cultural practices.

Regarding post-industrialism, alternatively known as deindustrialization, the tale begins with most Western countries' economies reaching the height of their industrial development by the 1950s: production of goods – actually making concrete products such as cars and tins of food – along with extractive industries such as mining, was the core economic activity much as it had been when Marx was setting forth his ideas on class a century before. The majority of the working population was therefore employed in the manufacturing sector, outnumbering those working in other sectors considerably and contributing to a certain (masculine) image of 'the working class'. After that, however, things began to change. The manufacturing workforce started to shrink as companies, taking advantage of technological advances and looser laws of corporate governance, either relocated their factories overseas to countries where labour was cheaper and less organized (especially the Far East) or replaced human workers with machines. In its place emerged the service sector – finance, media, tourism, research as well as personal services such as hairdressing, caring and catering – and by the end of the millennium the vast majority of workers across Western nations were service workers of some kind. In European countries, for example, the proportion of the workforce employed in services is now generally between two-thirds and three-quarters, while in the UK and the US the figure stands at around 80 per cent (Eurostat, 2013: 140; Lee and Mather, 2008) – far higher than the percentage employed in manufacturing even at its zenith. On top of that, developments in contraceptive technology and the emergence of feminism, coupled with the expansion of welfare, caring and clerical jobs demanding certain 'soft' skills (sociability, presentability and such like) disproportionately seen as feminine, vastly increased the numbers of women in paid employment, chipping away at the hard masculine image of the industrial working class.

Tied up with this shift was a decline of manual work across *all* industries. Having outweighed all other types of employment in the period leading up to the 1950s, by the start of the twenty-first century it had long been surpassed by clerical, professional and managerial positions. Western societies effectively moved from being comprised of a large manual workforce versus a smaller number of clerical workers and a tiny elite of bosses and professions (some depict this as like a pyramid) to comprising three fairly evenly spread categories of employment – manual, intermediate/clerical and professional-managerial (see Gallie, 2000; Breen, 2004). Along with this came a general increase in education and skill level within national workforces. In post-industrial economies revolving around provision of services and the production of knowledge rather than things, and with greater numbers of professionals and managers, obviously a larger section of the workforce required, and therefore acquired, what was previously an elite education, with post-compulsory and higher education expanding dramatically to cope with this. In fact even manual occupations often require recognized skills and certified training schemes nowadays.

Of course not everyone has benefitted from this – there are still divisions and inequalities in society – but it seemed as if 'class', a concept dreamt up a century ago, was no longer as useful for making sense of this as it once was. Instead what we had, said many, was a growing split between the majority of the population, on the one hand, who have some kind of education or training that guarantees them a stable and economically rewarding job, whether manual or professional – the 'contented majority', to use the term of the economist John Kenneth Galbraith (1992) – and a growing mass of people, especially in towns and cities hit hard by the decline of industry, without education, without skills and without full-time stable work as a result, on the other (Bauman, 2001). The latter, alternatively described as an underemployed 'underclass' or the 'socially excluded', apparently fall outside the logic of classes since they have no stable occupations, they produce nothing and are thus said to be literally 'under' the class system, not within it, yet they form one side of the key economic divide in society nowadays no matter what yardstick one wants to use (Gorz, 1982).

The second major development apparently undermining class is the emergence of neoliberalism, not least because it underlies in a rather shadowy way some of the other changes just described. Neoliberalism is an economic theory and a political philosophy – essentially a theory of how a government should run its economy if it is to secure a 'good life' for its citizens. From after the Second World War up to the 1970s most Western governments followed a different economic theory called Keynesianism, named after British economist John Maynard Keynes, which held that the best way to make sure capitalism works for all was for the government to intervene in the affairs of business, regulate and oversee them and limit what companies can do, to make the system fair, as well as spend money on the public sector to stave off recessions and depressions.

In the early 1970s, however, a colossal economic crisis forced governments in Europe and the US to look for new ideas, and the one which eventually won out was neoliberalism (see Atkinson et al., 2012). Neoliberalism holds that for markets to be successful in producing the best possible outcomes for everyone, they should be completely unregulated by the government – the government should back off, remove any restrictions on competition between businesses (because only through unbridled rivalry will you get real advances, innovation and economic growth) and leave the market alone. *Laissez faire*, as the French say. This included removing restrictions on the global mobility of businesses, which contributed to the deindustrialization already mentioned, as production moved overseas, and to the expansion of services, as big banks and financial service providers concentrated in major European cities such as London where they could have free rein to do as they pleased.

Neoliberalism also included removal of restrictions on labour policy. If a business is to be truly efficient, advocates of neoliberalism argue, if it is to respond to changing demands effectively and quickly, it needs to be *flexible*, i.e. to be able to expand, change and reduce its workforce as easily as possible – and not just at the bottom but at the top too, amongst management and professionals. In short, businesses have to be able to hire and fire people as they please, not get bogged down in employment law and employment tribunals discussing rights of dismissal, periods of notice and pay-outs. One consequence is that whereas people used to have a 'job for life', secure employment for the long term, now, the argument goes, they can be dismissed at the drop of a hat and they know it. Considering this can strike any position within the workforce, everyone apparently has more or less the same chances of being made redundant, of being on the scrap heap, of struggling to compete for new jobs, no matter what their skills or qualifications. Once again, therefore, the concept of class, or at least a certain version of the concept, supposedly ceases to be helpful here, since unemployment, career histories and workplace experience no longer run along its tracks (Beck, 2000; Bauman, 2001).

Finally, many of these changes were said to have transformed the cultural landscape of Western societies. Deindustrialization had dispersed the old working-class communities built around factories, mines, shipyards and the network of local pubs and clubs that sprang up around them, while rising incomes and availability of credit had opened up access to goods and lifestyle pursuits previously unattainable – more people can afford widescreen TVs, foreign holidays, fancy meals out and so on (Bell, 1979). Rather more contentiously, the distinction between the high culture associated with the upper classes and the popular culture of the working class was said to be breaking (or to have broken) down: everyone wears jeans, everyone watches football, football programmes use classical music as their theme tunes, professors listen to pop and rock music and so on (Crook et al., 1992). Finally, expanding media and advertising industries, with the help of new communications technology, bring all sorts of information and images from across the world into our daily lives, documenting and diffusing different ways of life (the Rio carnival, French literature, American films) and, so the argument goes, weakening the hold of family, friends, local community and work colleagues on our ideas, attitudes, tastes, mannerisms and interests (Giddens, 1991).

For a while in the 1980s and 1990s these changes and the arguments that went with them gave scholars of class considerable trouble. Many people turned away from the concept, chided it as out of date and chose to study other things instead. Postmodernists were the first and boldest among them – with one self-proclaimed postmodernist tract even audaciously titled *The Death of Class* (Pakulski and Waters, 1996) – but nowadays postmodernism seems like something of a moribund movement, its few genuine insights absorbed into mainstream sociology. A more recent threat to class research came from a collection of theorists who shy away from the excesses of postmodernism, and therefore maintain an air of greater credibility, but nevertheless suggest that the concept of class is somewhat *passé*. In its place, they argue, we should be studying 'individualization' or the increased 'reflexivity' of Western populations. The precise nature and meaning of these two terms differ according to the specific theorist, but the general idea is that, with neoliberalism, consumerism and so on, people are nowadays forced to think, reflect and be malleable when it comes to making decisions about careers, educational pathways, lifestyle preferences and so on. Once we could have relied on the traditions rooted in our local community or family relations, and therefore our class, or would have been hemmed in by constraints, but with these fast disappearing or transforming we now have no choice but to assess the new range of options in front of us and decide what is best for our own wellbeing and self-realization. Ulrich Beck (1992), Zygmunt Bauman (2001), Anthony Giddens (1991) and Margaret Archer (2007, 2013) are the most famous proponents of this view.

Until not long ago these ideas still seemed to cast a troublesome shadow over class analysis, especially in Britain, parts of Continental Europe and Australia – in the US, where New World individualism has long been the prevailing worldview, these claims hardly seemed new. Many class researchers were on the defensive, feeling it was necessary to justify why they were even doing what they were doing when dominant voices in sociology were telling them not to bother (see e.g. Skeggs, 1997; Marshall, 1997; Savage, 2000; Goldthorpe, 2007a; Crompton, 2008). Today, however, the trickiest times for the concept of class seem to be more or less over. Of course the global financial crisis of the late 2000s and the political measures of austerity which followed it both heightened awareness of continued inequalities and made the label of 'class' acceptable in wider political and sociological circles once again. Over time, moreover, the gross exaggerations, caricatures, flaky arguments and ungrounded assertions put forward by the theorists of individualization and reflexivity became more and more apparent (see Atkinson, 2010), raising doubts over their grand claims.

Yet the real boon to class analysis was its reinvention. Towards the end of the millennium, researchers of class in Europe and beyond, heeding advances in social and cultural theory, started to think about their concept in new ways.

Traditionalists were and still are resistant, but these innovative ideas shed fresh light on the changes of the twentieth century, casting post-industrialism, post-Keynesianism and consumerism not as nails in the coffin of class but as merely sources of transformation in how it works. Class inequalities and differences have not declined or disappeared in the twenty-first century, in other words, only changed their form – they may look very different from the past, but class structures, cultures, struggles and modes of domination persist as doggedly as ever. Certainly this is the case that will be made through this book.

Plan of the book

The first four chapters are going to track developments in *conceptualization*, or the main definitions of class on offer and their associated research programmes. We start first of all with Karl Marx and his current followers, particularly the American sociologist Erik Olin Wright, not just because Marx was the first to talk about class in a sociological way but also because in many people's eyes Marxism is the school of thought so closely associated with the concept of class that it almost seems to be conflated with it, as if the sociology of class and Marxism were one. To prove that assumption wrong we will then look at the writings of Marx's great rival in the sociology of class, Max Weber, and the most influential neo-Weberian around today, John Goldthorpe. Though the debate between Marxists and Weberians dominated the sociology of class for most of the twentieth century, however, they both appear to be on the decline, or at least on the defensive, as the newest generation of class researchers spearheading the reinvention of their focal concept has increasingly looked elsewhere for inspiration. In particular, the ideas of the French sociologist Pierre Bourdieu have captured the imagination – an advance for class analysis in my view, even if we have to admit there is plenty of room for further conceptual work – so a chapter will be dedicated to his work.

The first part will round out by covering one of the most intractable debates within class theory: the relationship between class and other sources of social division. Gender and ethnicity will be the focus here as they have generated the most literature and heated dispute, but age, disability and so on should also be borne in mind. I will examine how feminists and scholars of ethnicity have criticized class theory for overlooking the importance of their chosen topics, tie that critique to historical shifts in European societies and in theoretical priorities, and then look at how class researchers have tried to grapple with and overcome the issue. Feminists seem to have moved from a preference for Marx to a preference for Bourdieu in recent years, though not without some trenchant criticism of the Frenchman. As for class and ethnicity, Marxism is not so unfashionable, but there are strands of Bourdieu-inspired research which perhaps offer a way out of the impasse it seems to have found itself in.

Part II will then move on to review the key contemporary sites of class inequality, conflict and struggle. A range of research, trends and ideas will be looked at and linked to the theoretical outlooks covered in part I as well as broader debates over the nature of society, social change through the twentieth and twenty-first centuries, the health of class as a concept and its reinvigoration. Obviously a whole range of topics could have been looked at here, but I have whittled it down to four established, core areas of debate within class analysis. The first two of these are the related themes of social mobility and education, which have been particular preoccupations of neo-Weberian class research, though more recent Bourdieu-inspired work on mobility, schooling and childhood has started to have an impact. After that, chapter 8 will cover health inequalities stemming from class differences, reviewing the key ways of conceiving how they come about and offering something of a synthesis. Chapter 9, finally, will cover the relationship between class and politics and identities, the realm captured through questions such as 'what do people feel is important?', 'what are their interests?', 'what do they value?', 'where do they feel they belong?', 'with whom do they feel at home?' and 'how do they see themselves as different or similar – and as *superior* or *inferior* – to others?'. As in previous chapters, I will make the case that Bourdieu's approach, combining the material and the cultural elements of social life, offers the best way of making sense of the patterns observed and how they have changed over time.

Part I
Class Concepts

2
Class as Exploitation

Karl Marx may not have been the first to use the term 'class' in a social scientific way, but he has certainly been the most famous and, whether as direct inspiration or as someone against whom others feel the need to position themselves, the most influential. His views were worked out in the context of the rapid industrialization and turbulent politics of nineteenth-century Europe, and Marx spent much of his early life being chased across the continent by various authorities troubled by his radical journalism and political agitation. Eventually, in 1849, he settled in London, where he continued his usual political activism – participating in the establishment of the First International, an umbrella organization for a number of leftist political groups and trade unions – and the journalistic work that earned him his living. He also, however, spent large quantities of time sitting in the British Library undertaking the detailed research into economics and history that underpinned his masterwork, *Capital*, the first volume of which was first published in 1867.

Class was the linchpin of Marx's thought, that much is obvious. Yet it is fair to say that it is not always clear what exactly class *is* for him. The basic position – and the one that most people aware of Marx know – is that there are capitalists, or business owners, on the one hand, the proletariat, or workers, on the other, and that the first exploits the second. However, if we actually look at Marx's scattered writings, especially his analyses of particular historical events, whether in *Capital*, in short journalistic texts such as *The Eighteenth Brumaire of Louis Bonaparte* (Marx, 1852/1968) or in the many tracts he wrote with his friend and long-time collaborator Friedrich Engels, things are rarely that simple. The label of 'class' is applied to all kinds of groups of people that fail to fit the usual bill of exploited or exploiter – intellectuals, bankers, the petty bourgeoisie, the lumpenproletariat (Marx's term for the long-term unemployed) and such like. He also talks of the 'middle class' and the 'lower middle class' and multiple strata within the working class and so on. And of course Marx never himself outlined a formal, systematic definition of class – he *nearly* did at the end of the third volume of *Capital*, in the very last chapter, but he had the misfortune to die before he could write more than a few brief paragraphs.

This does not mean we cannot make sense of Marx's thought, though. We can piece together the fundamentals of his theory of classes, and to understand his use of the term throughout his work it is useful to distinguish, following Anthony Giddens (1981), a *general* model of classes, that is, Marx's abstract understanding of society and history as being constituted by the struggles between two conflicting classes, and his *concrete* analysis of classes in particular societies, where the picture becomes more complex.

The general model

Starting with the general model of classes, the fundamental point of departure is Marx's *materialist* view of humanity. The basic principle of the human condition, and therefore the driving force of human history, is not, for Marx, to be found in the realm of ideas or consciousness, as the idealist philosophy of Georg Hegel predominant in Germany in his youth had it, but the thoroughly practical business of working on nature and producing material goods such as food, shelter and clothing so that we can survive (Marx and Engels, 1845/1998). The relations involved in this productive work form the economic 'base' upon which all ideas,

culture and politics in a society are built like a vast superstructure, and it is through the way in which these relations are organized that social classes emerge, that struggle
occurs and that transformations of society take place (Marx,
1859/1968).

Specifically, each society is characterized by a principal
'mode of production' – a way of organizing the production
of material goods – and in any mode of production there are
always two fundamental classes defined by their contrasting
relation to the 'means of production', or the things which are
used to produce those material goods. To be more precise
there are, on the one hand, those who use the means of production to produce goods but do not own or control them
and, on the other, those who own or control the means of
production but do not engage in production themselves. In
contemporary Western societies since around the sixteenth
century, and in the vast majority of the world more recently,
the dominant mode of production has been capitalism, based
on the private buying, owning and selling of the means of
production such as factories, machinery, materials, land,
buildings and so on. The producers are the proletariat, or
more colloquially the 'working class' – the people who work
in factories making, designing and packing products, whether
they be beans, cars or jets, or outside of a factory building
houses or more factories – whilst the owners of the means of
production, of the factories and machines, are the capitalists,
or bourgeoisie.

The workers have to sell their labour to the bourgeoisie in
order to survive. In his earlier works Marx stressed the 'alienating' aspects of this process – the process of producing material goods, the most natural thing in the world, is no longer
controlled or dictated by the worker but by someone else
(Marx, 1844/1959). Later, however, he came to emphasize
the fact that the buying and selling of labour power, the
primary relationship between the bourgeoisie and the proletariat, is fundamentally a relation of *exploitation*. Marx's
reasoning here is steeped in the economic theory of his day,
drawing on ideas from David Ricardo and Adam Smith, but
the basic argument is that the capitalist extracts 'surplus
value' from the workers. Surplus value refers to the difference
between the value of what the worker is paid in wages (as

the means of reproducing their labour power – i.e. they can feed themselves and their families and therefore turn up to work the next day as well as provide workers for the future) and the value the worker produces for the capitalist in terms of goods. In other words, labour power creates more value than it costs to buy, and the capitalist can use that surplus not only to live but more importantly to buy further labour power and means of production (called capital accumulation). Think of a worker who operates a machine producing a particular item – perhaps clothes on a sewing machine – who is paid minimum wage, which at the time of writing is £6.50 an hour in Britain (and that is more than many business owners claim is necessary to reproduce that labour power, i.e. for workers to feed and clothe themselves well enough). Within that hour the worker may produce goods worth £20, and the £13.50 difference is the surplus value, which the owner then reinvests.

Let me emphasize at this point that class, strictly speaking, has absolutely nothing to do with prestige or income level as far as Marx is concerned. A highly skilled and highly paid worker may take home more money from their job than a fairly lowly capitalist makes and have a more lavish lifestyle to boot, but the fact remains that they are exploited by their employers whilst the capitalist is not, and therefore they remain within the dominated class.

Now the two classes of any mode of production, in capitalism the workers and the bourgeoisie, are always at the same time in mutual dependence and conflict. One cannot survive without the other – the workers need the capitalists to pay their wages, and the capitalists need the surplus value created by the workers, and if one class escapes the relationship then they are no longer a class as such. Yet they are also in conflict because their interests are in direct opposition: the workers are getting a bad deal because they should reap the value that they produce, but it is in the capitalists' interests that they do not, that wages are kept low and hours long so that as much surplus as possible can be squeezed out.

Inevitably, says Marx, the glaring contradictions of capitalism – the increased concentration of capital in ever fewer hands, the increased production of an ever larger reserve army of unemployed potential workers and so on – will push the proletariat to become conscious of its common situation and its objective interests. Its members will, as he puts it, become 'class conscious'. They will then band together and move from being what is often called (Marx himself did not use the term) a 'class-in-itself' – a collection of people in the same class situation – to being what Marx (1847/1955) called a 'class-for-itself' – a class fully conscious of its shared situation and grouped together to take action. They will eventually overthrow the capitalists, seize the state and abolish private ownership and control of property.

Until then, however, because the exploiting class, who are obviously the beneficiaries of the current system, are also always the politically dominant class as well, with the state acting as (in the words of Marx and Engels, 1848/1998) the 'executive committee' of the bourgeoisie, it seeks to transmit an *ideology* to the workers that legitimates and rationalizes the current state of affairs – that this is the best way to do things, that it is in their interests, that the free market is fair, that 'there is no alternative', that equality of opportunity is all we need and, most famously, that there is a heaven in which the sufferings of earthly life will be compensated (hence religion is 'the opium of the people'). When the workers are hoodwinked by this ideology and fail to see their real interests, they are said – not by Marx himself, who never used the phrase, but certainly by many Marxists – to be displaying 'false consciousness', and they develop 'class consciousness' when they throw this off, as they inevitably will.

The concrete analyses

So that, in a nutshell, is Marx's general theory of classes. Yet he recognized that things are never this simple in concrete reality and, in analysing particular events, he developed a few ways of acknowledging the co-existence of other groups and classes without compromising the general two-class image of society. In particular, he frequently drew attention to the existence of *transitional* classes and *subdivisions* of classes. The first includes two types of group, and relies on the fact that any change from one mode of production to the next, from feudalism to capitalism for example, happens not with a sudden bang but relatively slowly. Even when feudalism was legally abolished after the French Revolution in 1789, for instance, people and their practices hardly disappeared overnight. So we have, on the one hand, classes on their way *in* to existence but not quite forming one of the key classes yet – this was the case with the emergence of the bourgeoisie in feudalism, before capitalism became the dominant mode of production – and, on the other, those that are on the way *out* and no longer constitute a central class but still hang on into a new system of production – this is the case for the landed aristocracy, a hangover from feudalism who have persisted into capitalism in many nations. The second argument refers to the internal heterogeneity within any one class: different fractions have slightly divergent circumstances and interests but are still ultimately variations of their parent class. Perhaps the most obvious example is the petite (or petty) bourgeoisie, or small property owners, who work for themselves but have no employees, but Marx also distinguished various fractions of the working class who are exploited and immiserated to greater and lesser degrees – weavers, spinners, paupers and so on.

Both arguments might give room for considering the existence of a 'middle' class, such as the petite bourgeoisie in capitalism (which may include self-employed professionals), without the fundamental dualism being thrown out the window. Nevertheless, Marx claimed that the dynamics of capitalism – namely recurrent economic crises forcing people out of business and efforts to degrade working conditions for maximum profit – would eventually polarize society into two great camps, pushing everybody in the other groups and subclasses into either the shrinking capitalist minority or, more likely, the swelling proletariat majority. Self-employment would decline and professional jobs would be increasingly brought under corporate employment, stripped of their skills and routinized – a process subsequently called 'proletarianization'. Standing in stark opposition, these two camps would inevitably clash, resulting in nothing short of a total revolution ushering in a better world, namely communism.

Marxism in the twentieth and twenty-first centuries

When Marx died in 1883 his funeral was attended by only a small band of family and dedicated friends. Just thirty-four years later, however, the October Revolution in Russia led by Vladimir Ilyich Lenin established Marx's thought as a dominant force in global politics and set up the communism/capitalism schism that defined the Cold War years. Partly for this reason Marxism maintained only a tenuous hold on Western social science in the early twentieth century. In the United States, where the first academic studies of class (or its more innocuous-sounding cousin, 'stratification') were being undertaken, Marx was generally ignored or treated as an ideologue scarcely to be taken seriously, and other sources of inspiration – as we will see in the next chapter – were sought instead. What developments there were in Marxist theory, therefore, were usually undertaken by political theorists, philosophers and dissonant intellectuals in Europe. For example, György Lukács (1971), sometime communist politician and literary theorist, tried to redefine false consciousness in terms of 'reification', or being increasingly forced to see the world not as a fluid, organic whole but as so many discrete, mechanical, autonomous 'things' – including elements of one's own personality (loyalty, trustworthiness etc.) or skills. This, the logic goes, precludes a grasp of the capitalist system in its 'totality'.

It was only in the 1960s and 1970s that Marxism started to make serious inroads into university campuses in the English-speaking world, stimulated by the radical anti-capitalist spirit of the times observable in the worldwide strikes and student protests of 1968 and opposition to the Vietnam War. The trouble was, by then the changes and challenges of the twentieth century recounted in the last chapter had got under way and seemed to throw the applicability of Marx's characterization of classes into question. For one thing, for all the recurrent economic crises suffered, capitalism had not come crashing down in Western societies and the proletariat had not developed anything like class consciousness – where there were or are pockets of resistance, from the uprisings in 1968 through to the Occupy movement of the early twenty-first century, these have usually been led by students, intellectuals and bohemians. The proletariat, on the other hand, has actually become *more* integrated into the capitalist system than ever before – they are, in other words, working and living in it quite happily. This is generally held to have occurred through two processes. First, there was political incorporation: increasing participation in liberal democracy – the gaining of the vote, legalization and growth of trade unions, and emergence of representative workers' parties that could champion the interests of 'the working class' through negotiation and political debate – seemed to reduce the need for violent revolution and regime change (Dahrendorf, 1959). This 'institutionalization of class conflict', as it was called, hardly impressed Marxists since it rested on a narrow definition of working-class 'interests' and accommodation to capitalist exploitation and bourgeois institutions stacked against them. The second process – a particular preoccupation of the brand of Marxism associated with the Frankfurt School – was the co-opting of the working class into capitalism through the expansion of a consumerist ideology vaunting possession of accessible, but wholly unnecessary, material goods (fashionable clothes, new cars every year etc.) as the means to be 'free', to define oneself and to be successful (Marcuse, 1964).

Another factor said to be at odds with Marx's theory of classes was the emergence from the 1960s onwards of postindustrialism. The shift from manufacturing to services was, according to one prominent commentator, altering the face of division and conflict in society (Bell, 1973). With industrial workers rapidly making way for service providers, no longer was society fractured along the fault line of ownership and non-ownership of the means of production. Instead, the key source of domination, conflict and struggle was the divide between possessors and non-possessors of *knowledge*, or between experts of one kind or another and the rest of the populace. At the same time, in direct contrast to what Marx predicted, there was an explosion of occupations falling *between* the bourgeoisie and the dwindling proletariat strictly defined, even accounting for transitional classes and class fractions, including all manner of managerial, technical and professional positions.

A final issue was purely theoretical. Early interpreters of Marx, relying on the works that were available at the dawn of the twentieth century, stressed that absolutely everything boiled down to economic interests and struggles and, furthermore, that since social transformation was written into the laws of historical motion rather than carried out by active individuals, we could just sit back and wait for the eventual revolution to come. By midway through the century, however, this crude reductionism and determinism were proving both conceptually and politically bankrupt.

There were a number of ways in which Marxists tried to respond to these challenges. One approach was simply to say that critics were looking at the wrong level: post-industrialism, affluence and so on may have weakened class struggles *within* certain (i.e. Western) nation states, but on a *global* level class domination, exploitation and struggle persist as starkly and perniciously as ever. Immanuel Wallerstein's 'world systems theory' is perhaps the most well-known statement to this effect, but the efforts most explicitly concerned with rescuing the concept of class come from Leslie Sklair (2001) and William I. Robinson (2004).

Sklair talks in unequivocally Marxist terms about the existence of a new 'transnational capitalist class' (TCC) engaging in capital accumulation and exploitation across the globe, unattached to any particular nation state and pushing a worldwide consumerist ideology to sustain their profits. Ownership of the means of production around the world is still the defining characteristic, and any internal divisions (on grounds of nationality, for example) are secondary to the overriding collective interest in securing private property and squeezing out returns wherever they can. The argument comes a little unstuck, however, when Sklair then starts to try and give a bit more detail on what the TCC looks like and how it works. He identifies four fractions, *none* of which, it must be stressed, are necessarily direct owners of the means of production: corporate executives, global political elites, globetrotting professionals and the media. They are, for the most part, controllers of the means of production instead, which is, as we will soon see, a tricky definitional issue in itself. Sklair even recognizes that strict Marxists might find this classification unsatisfactory (if not downright contradictory), but stresses that if class theory is to survive it must acknowledge the existence of multiple non-economic forms of power and domination, and indeed the insights of other thinkers in theorizing them. That, of course, undermines the overt Marxist rhetoric, but also opens the door for rival schools of thought to assert that Sklair might as well go the whole way – after all, they will say, and as might become clearer over the next few chapters, their full insights give a better grasp not only of the internal struggles and divergent interests Sklair mentions within the TCC but of the nature and strategies of the TCC as a whole too, whether as a 'command bloc' (for Weberians) or a 'field of power' (for Bourdieusians).

Robinson is in fact critical of Sklair for precisely this reason and insists that the TCC, if it is to be a rigorously Marxist concept, must be defined purely in terms of ownership of the means of production. Yet he still then says the TCC is aided in its domination by global politicians without giving any consistent reason why, since the latter are not property owners, other than through an implicit economic reductionism, and he talks about the existence of a 'middle class' without any attempt to explore what defines it as such or what interests it possesses and struggles it partakes in. The problems of Marxism on the national level seem, all in all, to have followed it to the global level.

That being the case, then, how have other Marxists tried to make sense of the transformation of class relations *within* Western nation states? An early intervention, associated with the now-defunct Birmingham Centre for Contemporary Cultural Studies (CCCS), drew on the ideas of Antonio Gramsci (1891–1937), a Marxist political theorist who wrote his most important works while languishing in prison in Mussolini's fascist Italy. Gramsci (1973) had battled against the economic reductionism and simplistic view of ideological domination in mainstream Marxism by, amongst other things, emphasizing the need for cultural struggle – a battle of ways of life, or a 'war of position' as he put it – and pointing out that the ideas of the ruling class are best described as 'hegemonic', that is, dominant enough to constitute 'common sense' but not totally unchallengeable or without times of crisis. Gramsci still tends, like any other Marxist, to portray the ruling class as overly homogeneous and unified, but nevertheless the Birmingham school set out in the 1970s and 1980s to study the reconfiguration of class relations in post-industrial Britain, equipped with these insights. Their original project was to trace the rebirth of class struggle in a throng of rebellious youth subcultures such as Mods, Rockers, skinheads, punks and so on (see especially Hall and Jefferson, 1975/2006), but over time, as we will see in chapter 5, they became more and more interested in race and ethnicity and pushed class further and further into the background.

Others were more interested in trying to account for the new middling positions given Marx's prognosis of their decline and to map their place in relation to the two cardinal, fundamental classes. There were two different approaches to this. The first of these is called 'labour process theory' and was forwarded by the radical journalist Harry Braverman (1974). His basic thesis was that, yes, there has been an increase in non-manual, white-collar occupations, but a detailed analysis of their working conditions reveals that actually their work is being steadily 'deskilled', routinized and 'scientifically managed' by superiors, that is, broken down into component parts and steps that can be undertaken easily and repetitively by different people. Even managers and higher-level professionals are, in their turn, going to lose their autonomy and become deskilled workers under capitalism, essentially confirming but updating Marx's thesis of proletarianization. In academia, for example, the extent to which time and work practices are monitored and regulated by an expanding mass of managers with ever-more specific roles is a continuous and oft-satirized source of tension and concern. Labour process theory is still going strong in sociology, particularly the sociology of work, but it does rather ignore the issues of political and cultural incorporation and does nothing to counter the charge of economic reductionism.

The second approach was to try and elaborate a set of criteria that could establish where the new occupations sat in the capitalist system by looking at what features of the two main classes they possessed and, ultimately, which class they could be seen to belong to or be allied with. This gave rise to the so-called 'boundary debate' – the debate over where to draw the boundary between the proletariat and the bourgeoisie – that rumbled on between Marxists into the 1980s (see Abercrombie and Urry, 1983). One early contribution made the case that class positions are, according to Marx himself (and Lenin too), defined not just by ownership or not of the means of production but by their role in the social organization of the labour process, with some of the newer jobs – managerial and supervisory ones in particular – not necessarily being linked to ownership of property but still performing the 'function' of capital by being implicated in the oversight and control of the production process (Carchedi, 1977).

Another effort came from Nicos Poulantzas (1975), the key representative in class theory of the immensely influential but somewhat short-lived movement of 'structural Marxism' pioneered most famously by Louis Althusser. Structural Marxism tried to battle against economic reductionism by arguing that the transformation of nature for survival, which gives rise to economic relations, is only one form of practice we human beings engage in. We also have to engage in all sorts of activities aimed at organizing social relations – someone has to take charge and oversee how things work, who gets what and so on – and this gives rise to all the institutions and relations we think of as *politics* (especially the state and law). Moreover, human beings ceaselessly engage in activity aimed at understanding how the world works and how we fit into it, giving rise to all the institutions and relations involved in producing *ideology*, such as education and religion. Each of the three resulting sets of structures and relations, or 'instances' as Althusser put it, are 'relatively autonomous' from each other. Politics and ideology are not determined by the economy, they do not simply reflect it, they have their own internal logic and dynamic which can even affect economic relations, but the economy is still seen as the ultimate anchor of what goes on. The usual analogy here is with a factory or shop, which may have offices and 'research and development' departments with their own characters, office politics and debates over how to run the factory/shop, but these are still dependent upon and limited in what they can do by how the factory/shop works and performs.

Poulantzas tried to draw on this general logic to claim that class positions are shaped by not only economic factors but political ones – namely whether jobs involve supervision or not – and ideological ones – specifically whether their work is manual or 'mental' in character, with the latter supposedly involving access to knowledge of the production process. All three elements act as axes of class domination, and when taken together push the 'new middle class' of managers and experts into the same class position as the old middle class of self-employed entrepreneurs. Yet it was not much of a leap then to make the case that the ideological and political levels of society are actually *absolutely* autonomous from the economic level, and that, if it is no longer so important in the West anyway because of post-industrialism, we should really just forget about the economic level and concentrate on what is left: the new phenomena of political and ideological practice and domination, such as racism, sexism, ecological destruction and so on (Laclau and Mouffe, 1985). Thus was born one wing of the influential 'poststructuralist' movement in social theory – 'post-Marxism' – the consequences of which will resurface in more than one later chapter.

There was, however, one person who, while starting out from structuralist premises, refused to go along with the poststructural mood and insisted on the importance of class: Erik Olin Wright. He ended up taking Marxism in a radically different direction, and one perhaps as controversial and problematic as post-Marxism, but his initial entry point was his contribution to the boundary debate. In fact, Wright put forward by far the most influential solution to this particular dispute in the form of his famous notion of 'contradictory class locations' (Wright, 1978).

Contradictory class locations

In capitalism, Wright argued, there are three basic class locations forming a sort of triangle: the bourgeoisie, the proletariat and, between them, the petty bourgeoisie. The bourgeoisie are defined by the fact that they own and control the means of production and the labour of others, the proletariat by the fact that they do not own or control the means of production or their own labour, and the petty bourgeoisie (the self-employed) by the fact that they own their own means of production and control their own labour but do not control the labour of others.

But here is the thing, said Wright: in between each class position, along each of the lines connecting them, is a contradictory class location which contains elements of both of the classes it is between – they have 'a foot in both camps', as Harry Braverman once put it. First, managers and supervisors are in between the bourgeoisie and the proletariat because whilst, like the bourgeoisie, they control the means of production and the labour of others (making decisions, setting directives, disciplining), they do not own them, just like the workers. Next, in between the workers and the petite bourgeoisie are what Wright called 'semi-autonomous wage earners', who do not own the means of production, like the workers, but who do control their own labour, like the petite bourgeoisie. He was thinking here of high-skill jobs with some autonomy over what is done in a day's work – consulting occupations and professions (lawyers, doctors, professors), for instance. Finally, in between the bourgeoisie and the petite bourgeoisie are small employers, i.e. those who employ some but not a lot of people (figure 2.1).

As theoretically and pictorially neat as this may seem, however, problems soon emerged. The category of 'semi-autonomous wage earner', for example, is far too broad and vague. All kinds of different jobs can, following the criteria of inclusion, be lumped into this category which anyone, even a Marxist, can see have little in common – engineers and caretakers, for example. More important, though, was an issue Wright (1985) himself subsequently identified. This map of the class structure of advanced capitalist societies may well distinguish relations of ownership and control, decision-making powers and authority, but what has that got to do with *exploitation*? Surely any separating out of different fractions of classes or contradictory class locations has to be premised on different relationships to the extraction of surplus value? This is, after all, what defined class for Marx, not simply possession of property or how much influence one has. Knowing that, Wright conceded he would have to go back to the drawing board and come up with new criteria for making sense of today's array of occupations, and this he duly did.

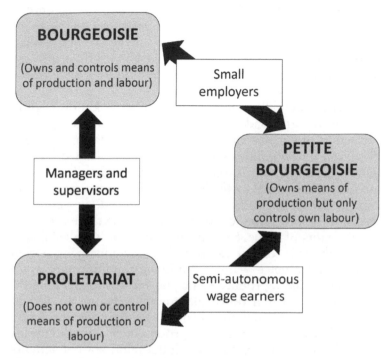

Figure 2.1 Erik Olin Wright's first class map
Source: Wright (1978: 63)

At first he distinguished a new set of categories on the basis of different co-existing forms of exploitation, drawing on the idea popular in structural Marxism that any concrete society can have more than one mode of production, and therefore mode of exploitation, operating at the same time (Wright, 1985). Later, however, he changed his mind and claimed we can make multiple distinctions within the propertyless class on the basis that some workers occupy what he calls 'privileged appropriation locations' within the capitalist exploitation relationship (Wright, 1997). Essentially what this means is that these locations, or people in these kinds of jobs, are paid more than the cost of reproducing their labour power, drawing therefore from the surplus extracted in the production process. Why is this so? In the case of managers and supervisors, they are paid more in order to secure their loyalty and their ability to maintain effectively and even improve exploitation (or as they see it, commitment to the 'goals of the company'). Wright calls this a 'loyalty rent'. Skilled workers and professionals are also paid more than the cost of reproducing their labour power because they have scarce skills, so they are paid a 'skill rent'.

Wright is actually using a notion of exploitation slightly different to and broader than the pure Marxist one based on extraction of surplus value. There are two reasons for this. First, Marx's definition is founded on the so-called 'labour theory of value', that is, the idea that the value of any commodity is determined by the labour power (measured in time) expended in producing it. This has proved, in economic terms, to be problematic, essentially because there are other determinants of value. Second, the notion of 'surplus' linked to the labour theory of value, and its accompanying notion of 'basic subsistence' – minimum living conditions necessary to maintain and reproduce labour power – are again remarkably difficult to nail down in economic theory. So Wright junks all this and says exploitation is simply the extraction of the 'fruits of labour' by one group which own the means of production from another which does not, but not actually extraction of surplus value in the strict sense given to that term in economics. In any case, these privileged positions within the propertyless class can still be considered contradictory class locations in the sense of being stuck between two poles of a relationship, but this time the relationship is one of exploitation. He also goes an extra step, however, and distinguishes multiple levels of loyalty rent and skill rent, though there is no rigorous theoretical reason given for cut-off points, yielding a system of twelve class locations (figure 2.2). The three categories on the bottom right – non-skilled workers, skilled workers and non-skilled supervisors – constitute the working class proper in Wright's eyes, while the rest of the contradictory positions he refers to as the 'middle class'.

Is this a credible updating and refinement of Marx's own thoughts on different class fractions? Perhaps, but many outside the Marxist camp would argue that some of the categories are still rather vague and allow some occupations to be slotted into places that seem to make little sense. For

Figure 2.2 Erik Olin Wright's second class map
Source: Wright (1997: 25)

example, a skilled machinist with an apprentice becomes a skilled supervisor, and therefore outside of the working class strictly defined, and a lorry driver with a driver's mate becomes a supervisor and is therefore assumed to have similar interests to others in that category (Marshall et al., 1988). Wright concedes that which occupations are allotted to which class hangs heavily on the way skill and authority are defined in any piece of research, but he has never provided any definitive criteria on this.

Marrying Marxism and bourgeois social science

Ending the boundary debate was not Wright's only motivation for working out this image of the class structure. From the start he was always concerned to make Marxism scientifically credible, that is to say, to convert people to Marxism not just for its political and moral commitments but on the basis of its strengths over other, rival theories of stratification as an explanatory framework making sense of research findings. Rather than reject what other Marxists often derided as 'bourgeois social science' and its methods, therefore, he decided to beat it on its own terms, primarily by carrying out surveys in which people's jobs could be assigned to the different class locations and then differences in all manner of outcomes and attitudes examined.

First there was his study of income determination, where he tried to prove that his earlier class map could better identify and explain differentials in income between jobs than rival images of stratification could (Wright, 1979), and then a study of proletarianization, where he noted a statistical decline since the 1960s in the number of people in contradictory class locations (Wright and Singlemann, 1982) – though this was later contradicted by subsequent research (Wright and Martin, 1987). Most importantly, however, Wright supervised a massive international research project called the Comparative Project on Class Structure and Class Consciousness (Wright, 1997). Spanning most of Europe, North America, Australia, New Zealand and much of Eastern Asia and taking nearly twenty years from conception to full reporting of results (in the late 1990s), this project investigated and compared the transformations in class structures, specifically which locations were becoming more or less numerous; the permeability of boundaries between class locations, in the form of not only mobility between locations over the life course and from generation to generation but likelihood of having friends and family from across different locations; the prevalence of class consciousness, as measured by indicators of attitudes towards capitalism, big business, trade unions, strikes – and so on. The point of all this, as with much of Wright's research, was to see which class locations were more likely to ally themselves with the proletariat and which with the capitalists in the struggle to bring about social change and equality.

In the meantime Wright has also been scrapping much of the traditional Marxist conceptual baggage (see especially Wright et al., 1992). We have already seen the labour theory of value underpinning the original surplus-value conception of exploitation dropped, but also, in advancing what he calls 'analytical Marxism' or, more prosaically, 'no-bullshit Marxism', Wright has severed his class scheme from Marx's theory of history – saying that social change is a probability, but not definite – and downgraded class from being the only important social division to being one amongst others, such as gender, which operate for the most part independently of class. Not even communism gets his full support any more – instead he has spent more recent years outlining his vision for a radically egalitarian, democratic society of the type that Marx himself might have dismissed (Wright, 2010). Finally, at one point Wright (1985) had flirted with the most bourgeois of all social sciences – game theory, or the conceptualization of social life as a series of 'games' played by rationally acting individuals concerned to maximize their outcomes – to make sense of exploitation.

Unsurprisingly, therefore, more orthodox Marxists have been critical of Wright's work (e.g. Resnick and Wolff, 2003; see also Wright et al., 1989). How can he be called a Marxist, or even, as he prefers to style himself, a neo-Marxist, when his fundamental economic, political and historical stance is so different from Marx's? Bring in the fact that Wright consistently puts so much emphasis on educational credentials and authority in determining class relations – which, as we will soon see, are more in line with Max Weber's views on class – and this prompts the charge that Wright is not actually a (neo-)Marxist in any real sense at all, but a Weberian masquerading as a Marxist (Rose and Marshall, 1986; Gubbay, 1997). 'Inside every Marxist', said Frank Parkin (1979: 25), a particularly caustic commentator, 'there seems to be a Weberian struggling to get out.' So while Wright may have tried to update Marxism, his critics say he has ended up leaving it behind instead – a symptom, perhaps, of any attempt to update Marxism and make it credible in today's world.

Wright (2005, 2009) has, however, responded by suggesting that actually, if you look closely, other definitions of class concerned with differences in education or skill are 'nested within' the Marxist one – in other words, Marxism can accommodate myriad distinctions and criteria for class, but it situates them within an overarching conceptualization of capitalism and exploitation. When others try to be a bit more radical and use their work to criticize capitalism they thus become, he retorts, Marxists masquerading as Weberians. Yet ultimately, he admits, it depends what questions you are asking your model of class to answer – if you just want to explain different life chances or cultural differences, then Marxism is not necessarily for you, but if you want to produce a critique of capitalism in the cause of emancipation, then Marxism is your best option. Some welcome this pluralism (e.g. Crompton, 2008), but it does imply Wright has given up trying to covert people to Marxism on the basis of its scientific credibility and explanatory power alone, relying instead on its political and moral dimension. Failing reason, then, this former prison chaplain plumps for faith. But this also does an injustice to other traditions of class research which do view capitalism as problematic and in need of challenge, or indeed overthrow, yet do not necessarily see exploitation as the definitive principle of class. Marxism does not have a monopoly on radical critique.

Conclusion

Marxism, once a fundamental force in class theory and research, is no longer as prominent as it was. It fitted the radical political spirit of the 1960s and seemed to make sense in a world dominated by the capitalism/communism schism, but when it came to nailing the theory down in deindustrializing consumer societies the problems soon stacked up, leading some to abandon all but the general critical ethos of Marx's analysis. Notwithstanding the German thinker's perennial influence on branches of philosophy and cultural theory and the efforts of some to shift the level of analysis to global goings-on, which only relocate the conceptual problems of Marxism to another echelon, the work of Erik Olin Wright remains the best-known sociological effort to rethink and refine (some would say water down) Marx's ideas. Whatever its conceptual issues, however, there is one quite telling fact: virtually no one uses Wright's class scheme in sociological research – even he has not used it for a while now. That is because the bulk of researchers interested in doing cross-national or comparative statistical analyses of class – the task for which Wright's model was devised – draw their inspiration from elsewhere and use rather different measures of class, as we shall see next.

3
Class as Life Chances

By the late nineteenth century, not long after he had died, Marx's ideas, at least as gleaned from the writings available at the time and their dubious interpretation and elaboration by defenders, had started to permeate the German intellectual world. The questions of capitalism's emergence and its features, of possible socialist or communist futures and of class interests and struggles had been raised and demanded to be taken seriously. Many scholars at the time, it is true, used them merely as foils for their own positions, but one man took a different approach – an approach which by turns praised Marxism and mocked it, recognized it as a vital contribution and lambasted its arguments, took on board some of its central themes while embedding them within a completely different approach to social science, so much so that commentators to this day argue over whether it represents little more than a 'sophisticated' or 'bourgeois' form of Marxism or a genuinely new perspective (Mommsen, 1977; Wright, 2002). This man was Max Weber, legal scholar, political theorist and pioneer of the discipline of sociology within Germany. Among his many and varied writings on this or that aspect of the social world is a sketch of classes and their place in capitalism – already a concession to the topics foregrounded by Marx – but one very different from what might be found in the pages of *Capital*, and one which subsequent sociologists have often preferred for a variety of reasons.

First of all, Weber gave a more rigorous and systematic theory of what exactly class is than did Marx, who shuffled off this mortal coil before he could really clarify his views, though even Weber's writings devoted to conceptualizing class consist of just two short essays in his masterwork *Economy and Society* (1978) which are not entirely consistent. There is also a sense in which Weber offers a more 'sociological' concept of class than did Marx, by which I mean one that was constructed out of and for careful observation and explanation, with its empirical and logical validity at stake, not one that was essentially conjured to express a speculative philosophy of history and frame the political project of a professional journalist and activist. This expresses a fundamental difference between the two thinkers: for Marx, social analysis was a means to bring about political change, encapsulated in his famous thesis that 'the philosophers have only interpreted the world; the point is to change it', whereas for Weber some level of value-freedom is necessary if we are to have adequate concepts and findings – so we do not let our values dictate our arguments – even if our choice of topic area is driven by value-relevant concerns.

Perhaps the most important reason why Weber is a preferred starting point for many sociologists, however, is that his theory of class manages to avoid many of the themes and concepts in Marxism which are seen as untenable, crude and unsatisfactory, and which have therefore, as we saw in the last chapter, occupied the minds of many a contemporary Marxist. For example, Weber does not, like Marx, tie social class to any theory of the inevitable progression of history. History is contingent and influenced by a multitude of interacting factors in his view, not determined, unstoppable and reducible to goings-on in the material realm alone. Whether and how class plays a role in social change is an empirical question, not pre-given.

On class consciousness, furthermore, Weber did not rule out the idea that those in the same class could become conscious of their common situation in a way similar to that proposed by Marx and pursue collective action and political organization, but he argued that this was not necessarily the case. It *could* happen given certain intervening social conditions, but it was not *bound* to happen simply because class differentiation exists, as Marx claimed. Third, though Marx admitted the existence of other classes in his concrete studies of historical events, as we have seen, these were still rather peripheral and his general model posited the existence of just two inextricably linked and conflicting classes in any mode of production. For Weber, on the other hand, this is not the case at all: there can be multiple classes in any one society defined in relation to a whole range of scarce resources. None of these are peripheral to the others, and whilst there is inevitably competition between classes, whether or not they engage in open struggle and conflict is, again, an empirical question – certainly it is not key to the very existence of the classes as classes. Lastly, Marxism has historically made little space for forms of social division and domination other than class, and this is basically because for Marx and Marxists class is the most fundamental social division and determines the way any other division, whether gender, ethnicity or whatever, works. Once again, for Weber this is not true: there are other forms of stratification and domination, and whilst these can interact with class they have their own, separate, autonomous dynamic. That said, Weber was certainly of the mind that societies can be classified according to their 'prevailing mode of stratification', and he was in no doubt that modern capitalism was a 'class society' through and through.

Class, status, party

So now that we have seen some of what Weber's theory of class does and does not assume, we can delve into the nuts and bolts of his argument. The fundamental starting point here is to remember that Weber was the original methodological individualist, so whereas classes for Marx sometimes seemed to have their own existence in the form of causal powers and interests over and above those of the individuals who make them up, for Weber they are, like any other collective entity, always reducible to the actions and properties of the individual human beings who make them up. Specifically, a class consists of a collection of individuals in a society who share what he calls a similar 'class situation', and by this he essentially means that these individuals have similar *rates* and *causes* of 'life chances'. Now 'life chances' is a fundamental term in class analysis and one that crops up all over the place, not just in sociology but also in policy studies and political debate. It basically refers to an individual's typical chance of obtaining that which is deemed desirable in a society – for example, quality housing, a decent education, social mobility, good health and even, in its most literal sense, life itself in the form of differences in mortality rates. Weber himself never actually charted differences in life chances, but just assumed them – all part and parcel of his methodology of constructing 'ideal types'.

If classes are defined by different rates and causes of life chances, then what determines someone's life chances? For Weber the key here is what he calls the individual's 'market situation', which means their capacity for securing income in markets of one type or another – what they can bring to the labour market or to the goods market to generate income. The fundamental division here, as for Marx, is the possession or not of property, though not because property holders exploit non-owners but because they have different types of resources generating different life chances. Also – and here is another break from Marx – on both sides of this divide, among the propertied and propertyless, there are further differences of market situations, life chances, class situations and thus classes (and not just class fractions). Amongst the property owners there are divisions based not simply on the size of the property, though that comes into it, but also on the type and use of property, including buildings, machines, livestock, slaves and such like. For example, Weber drew a distinction between the entrepreneur class – those who make money through production of goods or sales of services – and the rentier class – people who receive their income from rents of one type or another, whether from land and buildings or through copyright and intellectual property, as is the case today with computer software and music.

Amongst those who do not own property – those who must work for others and who make up the majority of the population – there is differentiation according to levels and types of skill and educational qualification. This is because different skills and qualifications are of different scarcity, and therefore value, putting their holders in different positions within the labour market (i.e. they can demand different levels of payment) and granting them different life chances. So unskilled workers (drivers, factory hands, cleaners), skilled tradespeople (plumbers, carpenters, builders) and degree-holding professionals (teachers, lawyers, doctors), for example, all have different market situations; they all therefore have different levels and causes of life chances, have different class situations and could even be considered separate classes.

Notice that when we are talking about classes here we are talking about them as objective, economic, structural features of society patterning life chances – people in a common situation, something like Marx's class-in-itself. How do we make sense, then, of classes as we actually experience them, as distinct, perceptible social groups, with communities, associated symbols, lifestyles, collective political interests and names that make no distinction between skilled and unskilled manual work or types of property – the 'working class', 'middle class' and so on? What is the link between this and economic classes? Weber has an answer, and it goes like this: people can end up forming these distinct, perceptible social groups, which he called *social* classes, when social mobility between particular class situations, whether over the generations or within one's own lifetime, is – in his words – 'easy and typical' yet social mobility beyond them into other class situations is less so. So, for example, skilled manual workers may, strictly speaking, have a different class situation from non-skilled workers, but because mobility between skilled and non-skilled work is statistically common and relatively straightforward, people in those occupations may tend to spend a lot of time together, interact together, form shared habits, customs and interests over time and so combine to form parts of the same *social class* – what people might call the 'working class'. On the other hand, because movement from skilled or unskilled work into medicine or law is relatively rare and hardly easy given the constraints faced (costs of study and so on), doctors and lawyers are in a separate social class from the (un)skilled workers, along with other professions – what people might call the 'middle class'. Weber (1978: 305) himself distinguished the working class, the petite bourgeoisie, the intelligentsia/specialists and the propertied class, the last actually being composed of the entrepreneur and rentier classes.

There is, however, another step here. It was mentioned earlier that Weber identified other forms of social division alongside class, and the most important of these is what he called *status*. This refers to the possession of different levels of prestige, honour or social esteem by groups in society, and this also confers power and life chances. The chief criteria for distinguishing status groups are (1) the possession of a common lifestyle – i.e. monopolization of certain practices and symbolic goods, from types of clothes or food to specific musical instruments – and (2) a degree of social closure – i.e. mixing and marrying only with those with the same lifestyle. Weber saw the feudal estates (the lords, peasants and bishops), religious groups, occupational groups, ethnic groups and castes as the main examples of his own day, but Pakulski and Waters (1996) have added that today's subcultures oriented around specific forms of music and ways of dressing (punks, Goths, skaters, hipsters and so on) can also be considered status groups.

Class and status distinctions do, however, interact and can even merge. Social classes, for example, can become status groups, so that members of the working class could be discriminated against simply because they are recognized as belonging to the working class. In the UK, for example, there is an almost annual scandal over the fact that the prestigious universities are stuffed with students coming from the elite fee-paying public school system (Eton, Harrow etc.) and turn down many from the state sector, despite their grades, on the basis of perception, stereotyping and assumptions of lifestyle differences (they are not 'like us'). Money is not the obstacle here. Nevertheless the two forms of inequality have their own separate dynamics: being high in status does not guarantee a great class situation; nor does being economically privileged automatically bring enhanced status, as denigration of the socially mobile or newly rich – as 'upstarts', 'social climbers', 'parvenu' or 'all money and no class' – attests.

Weber also referred to 'parties' in discussing the distribution of power amongst groups in society, but what he actually meant by this has been debated and differently interpreted.

It seems to refer to organized alliances set up specifically to pursue power and influence within some context, whether a state, a region, an organization or even a club of some kind, so they can include political parties (the most obvious example), trade unions, committees, congresses, associations and so on. They may represent the interests of a specific class or status group, or of a melange of classes and status groups, and mobilize a range of strategies, from violence and bribery to rhetoric and persuasion, to gain power. Parties of one sort or another, Weber stressed, existed in ancient and medieval times as much as today and are fundamental for understanding the sources of legitimacy and domination in any social order. Despite that, most scholars have tended to ignore or downplay this third module in Weber's triad of power distribution, and focus on class and status alone.

Class, capitalism and religion

For the most part Weber's writings on class are all about simply mapping the patterns of power in contemporary capitalist societies, but there are a few instances where he actually tried to put the concept to use, particularly in his comparative-historical sociology of religion. He is, of course, most famous for turning Marx on his head by arguing that it was the emergence of a particular religious credo, Calvinism, which underpinned, or at least was heavily implicated in, the transition to capitalism in Europe (Weber, 1905/2001). The basic argument was that Calvinism revolved around the doctrine of predestination, or the idea that God has already chosen whom to save from hellfire and whom to consign to eternal damnation, and there is nothing anyone can do within their lifetime to change this. However, because this was quite a terrifying principle, people were encouraged by the clergy to look for 'proof' of the fact that they were the chosen ones in their everyday lives, and there seemed no better proof than success in some particular calling or vocation. Success only came, however, with a certain mindset – careful use of time, avoidance of waste or excess and such like – and this lent itself rather well to enterprise and capital accumulation. In

other words the 'spirit of capitalism', or the bourgeois disposition to acquire private property and maximize profits, was
an unintended consequence of a specifically religious ethos.

In Weber's wider corpus on religion, however, the picture
is a little more complicated. He was no one-sided idealist –
more accurately, he thought it impossible to detect any one
overriding motor of historical development. Instead he was
interested in documenting the multiple, intertwining strands
that make up the complex tapestry of history and society,
meaning there are places where we can even find a relationship between religion and class, or a class/status fusion, that
is the apparent *reverse* of that at work in his thesis on the
Calvinism–capitalism connection; that is, an account of the
class/status origins of religious movements and the elements
of class situations inclining their incumbents towards particular creeds or styles of belief. In his famous section on the
sociology of religion in *Economy and Society* (1978: ch. 6),
for example, he pins the emergence of salvation-style religions
(i.e. religions with a vision of deliverance from sin and suffering) in all manner of societies, East and West, on the intel-
ligentsia, particularly as a compensatory or escapist response
to a loss of political power amongst the privileged strata of
society in the wake of bureaucratization of the state. Devalu-
ing all that is practical, physical and natural, they seek to
infuse their world with a deeper meaning and embed it in the
workings of a transcendent deity, opposing the animism,
belief in magic and preference for local idols of the peasantry
and lower strata. This is part and parcel of Weber's broader
thesis of the 'disenchantment' of the world – not through
secularization, but, at least at first, through the emergence of
a more rational, 'centralized' religious worldview.

However, while the salvation religion picks up followers
from other classes it does so only in so far as it fits their different interests and undergoes some degree of transformation.
Amongst the privileged, salvation religion provides *legitima-
tion* or *justification* for their privilege and happiness: their
'success' in life compared to others fits in with a higher plan.
Amongst the less privileged classes and status groups, on the
other hand, salvation religion acts as a form of *compensation*:
while they may not be able to gain esteem or advantage on
the basis of what they *are* in this world, they can instead find

worth in what they are fated to *become* in the afterlife, where a divine authority offering a different 'scale of values' to that imposed on them in life accords them everlasting significance. Not only that, but the nature of the religion tends to mutate: lower down the social order, where economic security is scarcer and there is a closer attachment to the folk beliefs derived from working with nature and craft traditions (and, of course, where there is less of an intellectualist interest in transcendence and abstraction), there is a need for some concrete and embodied 'saviour' to whom hopes and praise can be attached, as well as canonization of local deities with a greater practical significance. All very well; but one cannot help but wonder whether Weber is beginning to overstep the explanatory capacity of his own concepts of class and status here, since the described connections between social positions and religious dispositions seem to go beyond the strict logic of life chances, and whether we may have to look elsewhere to fill in the gaps.

After Weber

After his premature death in 1920, Weber was influential in the earliest sociological studies of class in the United States – such as William Lloyd Warner's multi-volume ethnography of 'Yankee City' – and, through the medium of Talcott Parsons, in the famed functionalist approach to stratification put forward by Davis and Moore (1945). Usually, however, the influence was partial and, thanks to the fact that Parsons' somewhat slanted translation and interpretation of Weber was the only one available for a while, rather distorted. Occupational groups were generally distinguished on the basis of their prestige levels rather than their life chances, for example, yet named 'classes' rather than status groups, and the economic dimension tended to get sidelined, with income peripheral to status. Later researchers added income and education to the mix, laying the groundwork for the vague and uncertain multidimensionalism which survives to this day in the notion of 'socio-economic status' popular in economics, psychology, epidemiology and policy studies.

Through the 1950s, 1960s and 1970s, however, Weber's own views were better translated and opened up to new interpretations, with many beginning to call themselves Weberians or neo-Weberians explicitly and spend their time trying to elaborate and defend his position. Some, such as Frank Parkin (1979), Raymond Murphy (1988) and Randall Collins (1979), followed up on Weber's scattered remarks on 'social closure' to explore the ways in which specific social classes (in Weber's sense) constitute themselves by hoarding resources and opportunities, excluding others and closing ranks. John Scott (1996), moreover, has tried to supplement Weber's writings on class and status by reinterpreting the brief writings on 'parties'. If 'class' refers to economic situations and 'status' to prestige, he says, then this third dimension should be conceived in terms of positions of *authority* or *command* in institutions, whether they be in the state and public organizations, private companies or churches and charities. These positions also confer different life chances, he says, and mobility can be easy and typical between them: people moving from senior positions in government to the private sector to sitting on boards of charities etc. – just like Tony Blair, the former UK prime minister, who after leaving office took up positions advising the investment bank JP Morgan and the financial service provider Zurich as well as setting up his own faith-based charities. Just as class situations can act as the basis for social classes, then, Scott argues that these positions can aggregate to form social blocs or 'elites' which are separable from but interact with classes and status groups. This is not empty theoretical speculation either – Scott has undertaken plenty of historical research on 'who rules Britain' (Scott, 1991).

The Nuffield School

Without a doubt, however, the most influential contemporary neo-Weberian today is the British sociologist John Goldthorpe. When he set out his current position he was associated with the Nuffield programme of research into social mobility – so called because of its association with Nuffield College at Oxford, where Goldthorpe has spent most of his career and is emeritus professor today. Sometimes the approach of Goldthorpe and his colleagues is thus called the Nuffield approach or Nuffield School. Goldthorpe himself refers to his vision of the class structure as the 'EGP scheme', named after himself (the G) and two other colleagues with whom he developed it – Robert Erikson and Lucienne Portocarero.

Only recently, in fact, has Goldthorpe stopped denying attachment to any particular theoretical heritage, but Weberian presuppositions were fairly clear from the start. To begin with, like Weber, Goldthorpe does not see class as tied to any theory of history, and has actually been a severe and incessant critic of those who see history as having some form of direction – including Marxists but also functionalists and others who see industrial capitalism as the logical end phase of history because it cannot be surpassed. Having said that, he then departs somewhat from Weber in arguing that even questions concerning how the class structure came to be as it is today lie outside the scope of class research – that is for historians to muse over. Second, Goldthorpe has always tied the concept of class and his research to the idea of uncovering patterns of life chances. Third, like Weber (and of course Wright nowadays), Goldthorpe sees class as not the only or even the most important source of division and inequality in society: even though that is what he has chosen to study for most of his career, how important it is, he claims, is an empirical question. Last, as we will see, Goldthorpe's understanding of class is based on relationships in the labour market, just as Weber's was.

So what is the logic of Goldthorpe's definition of class? Originally, when he initially forwarded his ideas in 1980, the underlying premise was the clustering together of occupations into distinct classes on the basis of two features: their 'market situation' and their 'work situation'. The terms were taken from an earlier study by David Lockwood (1958), a celebrated British conflict theorist, but obviously the link to Weber (via market situation) is clear. That said, Goldthorpe's definition was slightly different from Weber's: he understood market situation to mean the source and level of income, economic security and chances for economic advancement (i.e. pay increases with career progression) associated with an occupation, not an individual, as he is interested in the slots into which people fall, not the people themselves; and he added 'work situation', which Weber did not mention, to refer to a job's level of authority and control in the workplace (cf. Dahrendorf, 1959). Where occupations were similar, or in his words 'typically comparable', with respect to these, they could be grouped together into a class, and in fact he identified seven such classes in Britain – a far cry from Marx's two.

Goldthorpe has, just like Wright, since changed the under-pinning logic for differentiating classes, arguing that his previous criteria were too focused on features of work rather than economic relationships and situations, but the end result is exactly the same (Erikson and Goldthorpe, 1992). To pull out the different classes now, Goldthorpe distinguishes between two types of *employment relation*, or two ways in which jobs are provided by employers, the understanding being that these provide constraints or opportunities for action and therefore shape life chances. On the one hand, there are those occupations that involve a 'labour contract', where there is a simple short-term exchange of reward for labour on a piece or time basis and no promises are made beyond that – i.e. one is paid a specific rate per hour (£7 an hour, say) or per job or item (piece of clothing, a house exten-sion and so on). This is more characteristic of manual work. On the other hand there is a 'service relationship', where the employee is remunerated not just with a salary and perks, but with *prospective* rewards including promised pay increases and promotion options, making the employment relation much more long-term.

Why do some occupations have a labour contract and others a service relationship? This comes down to two things, says Goldthorpe (2007a): on the one hand, the *specificity of human capital*, by which he means, like Weber, the distinctive-ness and rareness of the skills and capacities which that job requires (a degree in sociology, a higher vocational qualifica-tion in engineering etc.); and on the other hand, *difficulty of monitoring* – that is to say, the extent to which the produc-tivity of an occupation can be easily measured quantitatively or qualitatively. Measuring the number of clothes produced or bricks laid is fairly straightforward, but cases won by a lawyer, research done by a professor, the performance of a manager are harder to measure on a like-for-like basis – that does not stop people from trying, but it is still qualitatively different to the supervision of those on a labour contract. With high specificity of skills and difficulty of monitoring you get a service contract, essentially in order to secure commitment; with low specificity and low difficulty you get a labour contract. Goldthorpe also recognized that some occupations have a mixture of the two forms of employment relationship, and that some have modified versions of one or the other. The result is the class scheme, or map, in table 3.1.

Table 3.1   Goldthorpe's class scheme

Aggregate class	Class	Description	Employment relation
Service class	I	Higher-grade professionals and managers; large proprietors	Service relationship
	II	Lower-grade professionals and managers; higher-grade technicians	Service relationship (modified)
Intermediate class	IIIa	Higher-grade routine non-manual employees	Mixed (high difficulty of monitoring, low specificity)
	IIIb	Lower-grade routine non-manual employees	Labour contract (modified)
	IV	Small employers and proprietors; self-employed workers	Self-employed
	V	Technicians; supervisors of manual workers	Mixed (low difficulty of monitoring, high specificity)
Working class	VI	Skilled workers	Labour contract (modified)
	VIIa	Non-skilled workers (industrial)	Labour contract
	VIIb	Agricultural workers	Labour contract

Source: Goldthorpe (1987: 305). By permission of Oxford University Press.

The three 'aggregate' classes within which the class categories sit are not *social classes* in the sense of distinct social groups – they are simply ways of combining smaller classes to deal with low numbers in statistical research. The most famous of these aggregate classes, and certainly the one Goldthorpe (1982, 1995) has spent most time reflecting on, is the 'service class' (sometimes also called 'the salariat') composed of managers, higher-level administrators and professionals. Note, however, that class I also includes large employers, so for Goldthorpe what Marxists would see as the bourgeoisie and in a class of their own can actually be treated as just a small part of one class among many. Obviously there is no employment relation here since they are employers, so they are simply put there because they are judged to have similar life chances to the professionals. The self-employed also form their own class and sit where they do in the hierarchy on the basis of their assumed rate of life chances.

The Nuffield research agenda

Goldthorpe's class scheme was designed specifically for the purposes of empirical (more specifically, statistical) research. People are assigned to classes in large-scale surveys on the basis of their occupations and then this can be run against data on all kinds of things to see what the impact of class is. What the Nuffield programme is best known for is its analysis of social mobility, covered in chapter 6, but the theoretical backdrop to these studies is worth just mentioning here. At first Goldthorpe (1980) actually followed the Weberian agenda of studying mobility rates to see whether they were restricted to certain local areas within the class structure, and therefore whether *social* classes in Weber's sense were likely to form and become politicized in some way. Since then, however, Goldthorpe's interest in class formation has waned. He is still very much interested in social mobility, but now more as an indicator of how 'open' society is – if it is fully open, as some claim it is, then class is no constraint and there should be absolutely no correlation between one's father's class and one's own. Needless to say he has found it wanting in this regard, primarily because if you really want equality of opportunity you need to have, he says, equality of condition (i.e. redistribution of wealth and equal pay).

There are other themes Goldthorpe and his colleagues have looked at, including: voting patterns, to test whether class is an important factor in political change; class identities and attitudes, to see whether belonging to a particular class position affects one's self-perception and perception of social and political issues, though these phenomena are deemed peripheral to the definition of class and no real proof of its importance; and a lot of other indicators of life chances such as educational success or health which we will examine in greater depth later. Indeed, Goldthorpe's class scheme has been so popular, and so easily reproduced in research, that it has now been adopted in only a very slightly modified way as the UK government's own official measure of class in its research: the National Statistics Socio-Economic Classification, to give it its full name, or NS-SEC as it is called for short. Goldthorpe's definition of class is, therefore, the officially sanctioned one. Not only that, but there has more recently been development of a Europe-wide class categorization following the same logic, called the ESeC, used for comparative research (Rose and Harrison, 2011).

Criticisms of the Nuffield School

There is no doubt Goldthorpe and his colleagues have been immensely influential and successful in making class a topic of rigorous social research. Before they came along there were few adequate measures of social class for doing research on international or even national patterns and inequalities, only administrative or market research measures based on little if any theoretical reasoning. That does not mean, however, that his approach is faultless or without its critics. Far from it: as soon as he formulated his ideas there was criticism, and this has steadily accumulated over the years to form a weighty catalogue of dissatisfaction.

First, argued some, as his research progressed and his taste for rather advanced statistical analysis increased, particularly logistic regression, Goldthorpe's class analysis was in danger of becoming a rather narrow, or 'attenuated', undertaking consisting of improving the performance of statistical variables (Ahrne, 1991; Morris and Scott, 1996). This was epitomized by a controversial paper by Goldthorpe and his colleague Gordon Marshall (1992) in which they explicitly rejected the need for any particular theoretical justification of class analysis – the class scheme is a research tool, they said, and the ultimate criterion for differentiating classes is the ability to pick up the maximum differences in life chances.

In response, just as Marxists chided Wright for dropping too much Marxism, Lydia Morris and John Scott chided Goldthorpe for losing sight of his Weberian roots, forgetting his interest in the formation of social classes, stripping class of its explanatory role in historical change and conflict and effectively reducing the concept to a list of arbitrary and nominalist categorizations of occupations. It was *arbitrary* because if class is to be defined in terms of differentiating life chances, then why stop where he has and not refine them even further? (This was before Goldthorpe's elaboration of why there are different employment contracts, which might be considered something of a post-hoc theorization.) Indeed, quite a few people, including many who are sympathetic to the broad thrust of Goldthorpe's approach, have argued that the service class is too undifferentiated. We may well have a higher and lower fraction in Goldthorpe's scheme, but evidence stubbornly tends to show that there are significant differences of one sort or another, with real empirical manifestations, between those with high levels of education, who tend to work in the public sector, and those earning fairly well in the private sector but not necessarily highly educated, such as managers and business leaders (Savage et al., 1992; Esping-Anderson, 1993; Evans, 1999; Houtman, 2003; Güveli et al., 2007). Goldthorpe (1982, 1995) himself claims that this boils down to 'situs', which means differentiation of occupational groups by function or industry rather than class, but education level seems to be key, and from a strictly Weberian point of view – indeed, in line with Weber's own list of classes in capitalism – this could be considered a significant differentiator of market and class situations.

The class scheme was *nominalist*, Morris and Scott continued, because Goldthorpe's 'classes' exist in name and on paper only – they do not correspond to real, experienced social divisions or groups, i.e. social classes, at all. This ties in with a criticism coming from a slightly different direction – from the 'cultural class analysts' covered in the next chapter, to be precise (e.g. Savage, 2000): the Nuffield School's neglect of class *culture*, not only in their particular research programme but in the very definition of class. The fact is, say the cultural class analysts, clashes and struggles over the right way to live, over what is legitimate in matters of cultural taste or childrearing and what is not, are fundamental to understanding what class is and how it works, yet exploration of these themes is generally beyond the capacities of Goldthorpe's class scheme and, in any case, they hardly match up with his neat little boxes designed for statistical purposes. People do not even have to have jobs to be implicated in cultural struggles between classes.

Last, it was also noted in the early 1990s that Goldthorpe lacked any real theoretical reasoning on the connection between the constraints of class and the social action which underlies the statistical patterns revealed by his research (Johnson, 1991). He showed all these patterns and hypothesized the constraints and opportunities, but he failed to offer much explanation as to how individuals actually make sense of these constraints and adjust their action accordingly. In Coleman's (1986) terms, he seemed to describe the relationship between one 'macro' phenomenon (class) and another (rates of mobility and life chances) without specifying how this works at the 'micro' level of individual action – a strange position for someone supposedly inspired by the ultimate methodological individualist.

Deepening the debt

Goldthorpe has a tendency to be fairly combative, but he has heeded these criticisms implicitly by deepening his debt to Weber in two ways. First of all, he and many of those influenced by him now advocate a version of rational action theory (RAT) to explain the statistical patterns they uncover. People are, in effect, acting to maximize outcomes in the face of the constraints and opportunities associated with certain class positions when they decide, for example, to get a job rather than go to university. True, his view actually owes less to Weber than to other theorists of rational choice here, including economists, philosophers and other statistical researchers who have a liking for it, but Weber is famous for his analysis of instrumental-rational action in contemporary society, so the connection is certainly there.

Second, in response to criticisms of his lack of attention to culture and his weakening ties to his Weberian roots, Goldthorpe has more recently embarked, with his colleague Tak Wing Chan, on a theoretical and empirical rejuvenation of the concept of *status* (Chan and Goldthorpe, 2010). They define it very differently from Weber, though – a status group is essentially a collection of occupations which are clustered together on the basis of *differential association*. So, for example, lawyers are likely to associate with (be friends with, marry etc.) doctors but not plumbers and so can be seen to be in the same status group as the former but not the latter. Chan and Goldthorpe have compared it with class in terms of the effects on attendance at different cultural venues, such as galleries, dance events, musical events and so on, and found that status has by far and away a greater impact on attendance and non-attendance. On the basis of this research they effectively reject the idea that classes correspond to or have any effect on cultural practices and tastes, but argue that there are distinct status groups in contemporary Britain, ulti-mately based on different 'information processing capacities' (the higher one's processing capacity, the more likely one is to desire 'complex' forms of culture such as classical music or modern art). Unsurprisingly the status groups thus corre-spond fairly closely to education level.

Both developments, however, are problematic. On the one hand, RAT suffers from the not insignificant setback that it is not a very realistic picture of how human beings actually behave – and even those otherwise sympathetic to Goldthorpe's general programme admit that (e.g. Hedström, 2005). It might be a nice *rationalization* of statistical patterns and trends, but it has very little phenomenological validity in the sense of fitting how people actually see and act in the world – not that Goldthorpe or anyone at Nuffield has examined the phenomenology of class lately. The two equally awkward responses to this are either (1) to say that hardly matters and prioritize the elegance of one's model by reducing people to calculating machines, with no control over their behaviour or knowledge of why they do what they do – in the style of arch-rational choice theorist Gary Becker (1978) – or, as Goldthorpe himself sometimes tends to do, (2) to water down RAT in the hope of making it more realistic by bringing in all sorts of non-rational factors until RAT loses its distinctiveness – a drowned RAT, if you will. In any case, the main point of opposition to it from other class researchers is that it fails to take account of the fact that what is considered 'rational' in any class position is not simply a utilitarian matter of material costs versus benefits but is, instead, embedded in class cultures – that is, unspoken expectations, tacit norms and taken-for-granted evaluations (Devine, 1998; Savage, 2000).

As to the separation of class and status, there are issues with the way status is conceptualized and operationalized: being based on occupations, it squeezes out ethnicity, for example, which was a key example of a lifestyle or status group for Weber. If anything, since it relies on differential association, it seems more like *social class* in Weber's sense than status groups per se, but Goldthorpe certainly does not see them as such, and if they were then it would be odd to sever them from economic classes. There are also issues with the way Chan and Goldthorpe go about researching cultural differences: for them it is all about what someone is seen doing in public, such as going to the theatre or cinema, rather than the tastes which underlie those excursions and which might differentiate varying ways of consuming the same thing. The biggest challenge to the programme of research on culture, however, is the contention that class and status are not actually separable at all, and that Goldthorpe can only say they are because he has an exceptionally narrow and inadequate definition of class to begin with. The basis of this claim we will explore next.

4
Class as Misrecognition

For a long time, i.e. from the end of the 1970s, Erik Olin Wright and John Goldthorpe were the major players in sociological research on class. They cornered the market in terms of publications, research projects, textbook discussion, followers and influence. There was, to be fair, a third strand of work in Britain called the 'Cambridge school', which emerged about the same time and argued that classes should be defined and measured in terms of friendship clusters much as Goldthorpe argues of status (Stewart et al., 1980), but, notwithstanding one or two important advocates in more recent years (e.g. Bottero, 2005), this has always been a little marginal. From the mid-1990s, however, things started to change, primarily because of accumulated dissatisfaction with the limits of Wright's and Goldthorpe's approaches. Both, for one thing, came to prominence privileging statistical research – assigning people to a class category on the basis of characteristics of their occupation, asking them survey questions on whatever topic, and then correlating the results or using some other statistical procedure. Now this is all very well, but critics noted two things.

First, debates over class were starting to become debates over the correct statistical procedures to use and how to construct and refine variables adequately, and because these required specialist training it was making class theory and research a little inaccessible to those not directly studying

class but potentially interested in it, feminists and practition-
ers of cultural studies prime among them (Savage, 2000).
Indeed, this was partly responsible for turning many social
and cultural theorists away from class altogether in the 1980s
and 1990s. Second, there is a limit to what quantitative
research can investigate – it cannot, for instance, provide any
real insight into the way class is *lived* and *experienced* in
everyday life, or what 'class' actually means to people, or how
it affects how people relate to and judge one another on a
daily basis. For Goldthorpe and Wright all this is unimportant anyway and hence no great loss, but for others these
themes *are* important, if not central, to the sociological study
of class because they get at the real emotional and existential
pain that can attach to routine classed experiences.

Another point of dissatisfaction, as we have already seen,
was the rational action model of human beings that both
theories appealed to (temporarily for Wright, to this day for
Goldthorpe); that is, the idea that human action can be
reduced to cost–benefit analysis in the pursuit of maximum
gain. The driving criticism was that rational actor models,
invariably imposed on statistical patterns by sociologists from
afar (putting the head of the sociologist on the body of the
average citizen), ignore the importance of unspoken expectations and tacit values embedded in the material and cultural
conditions of life of different classes, demonstrated with qualitative research that actually investigates people's decision-
making processes in detail. This in turn points to the broader
dissatisfaction with Goldthorpe and Wright's unwillingness
to study class *culture*, and the inability of their theories to do
so even if they were willing. Inequalities of life chances are
obviously important and need investigating, but Goldthorpe
and Wright tend to miss the way in which cultural traits –
lifestyles, behaviours and so on – are not only inherently
bound up with class but differently *valued*, with some being
denigrated and painted as problematic in the media, politics
and everyday life, creating feelings of inadequacy, inferiority,
shame or guilt amongst those who perceive themselves as the
targets, while others are praised and aspired to.

With the Wright–Goldthorpe dominance cracking, a whole
host of alternative approaches to class began to spring up
around the millennium and struggle for position. One strand

of work, pioneered by David Grusky (2005) in the US, has called for a 'Durkheimian' reorientation of the concept away from large classifications and towards the analysis of smaller clusters of occupations (or 'micro-classes') on the basis of their place within the technical division of labour, since these are so much closer to our everyday experience of social solidarity and cultural identity. However, by far the most influential new perspective, pioneered in the UK but with allied strands of work across the globe, is what some have called 'cultural class analysis' (Savage, 2003). There are quite a few people huddled under this heading, and they all have their own particular research programmes and agendas, but the common starting point is the often misunderstood class theory of Pierre Bourdieu, who first began working out his ideas on class some time before Wright or Goldthorpe but for many years remained less known for these than for his particular writings on education or anthropology. Like Wright or Goldthorpe, the cultural class analysts have often given the impression that they are inspired by or oriented towards the concerns of the body of thought on which they draw without being committed to its full baggage. Unlike Wright or Goldthorpe, however, they have, as yet, added very few conceptual innovations of their own. Most of the advances, and the way in which they have reinvigorated the study of class, have come through empirical research on areas not necessarily explored by Bourdieu himself, or explored by him a long time ago. Much of this work will crop up in later chapters, so for now we can content ourselves with getting to grips with the core features of Bourdieu's own approach to class.

The social space

The fundamental starting point is this: class is not simply about life chances, even if they do come into it, nor is it about exploitation, even if that does follow from it. Instead class is about the fundamental principles of social and cultural difference within a society, the different conditions of life tied up with those differences and the power, struggle and domination invested in them. Ultimately this is grounded in a contrasting conception of human nature to the Marxist one. For Marx, *Homo sapiens* is first a producer, transforming nature to meet the needs of her own and others' survival, but for Bourdieu (1990a, 2000), linking up in many ways with the critical theory of Axel Honneth (1995), there is something which comes before this: the need and desire to be *recognized* by others, in the sense of having some kind of worth and value in the eyes of others, so as to bestow justification on our existence. Without some degree of mutual recognition, no productive relations can be entered into. However, the seeds are always there for recognition to be at the expense of others. This is because to be seen as worthy or valuable inherently involves struggling to be seen as worthier and more valuable *than others*, which entails appropriating and monopolizing certain capacities and properties, working to get them perceived as unquestionably legitimate – and thus *mis*recognized by people since this masks the arbitrary and power-laden nature of those capacities – and explicitly or implicitly putting down, denigrating or dominating (including by exploiting) those without them. These capacities and properties Bourdieu, playing off of Marx, calls 'capitals'.

In contemporary capitalist societies, says Bourdieu, we can identify three major capitals. First, and perhaps most fundamentally, there is economic capital, which includes one's total wealth, income and property ownership all taken together as one measure. Second, there is what he calls cultural capital. This is a famous and much misunderstood term, and it is certainly encompassing, but at root it refers to all that which is usually described as 'intelligence' and is, therefore, measurable through educational qualifications. It includes a certain mode of using language, i.e. having an elaborate, extended vocabulary and 'correct' grammar, but more generally it refers to a capacity to articulate and formalize abstract principles of, and logical relations between, items and experiences in the world, whether in relation to art (e.g. recognizing an artwork as Impressionist), the natural world (e.g. linking one's behaviour to global warming), social relations (e.g. seeing a politician's speech as 'ideology' in action) or whatever. Bourdieu called this 'symbolic mastery' because it involves having some kind of handle on abstract symbolic systems (art history, scientific theories etc.) and locating everyday experience within them – a capacity which is ultimately only one way of knowing the world but which is accorded high value. Third, Bourdieu also mentions social capital, which refers to resources based on our social networks and association with particular names, clubs and families. These too might open doors, get us special treatment and so on. Bourdieu does also mention a fourth capital, called symbolic capital, but actually that refers to all the other capitals when perceived as legitimate and, therefore, granting authority or recognition. So economic, cultural and social capital are all forms of symbolic capital – they only work, and confer authority, opportunities and life chances, in so far as they are generally (mis)recognized as legitimate.

People possess different levels and combinations of capital, but instead of being positioned within a set of categories or layers on that basis, as they would be for Wright or Goldthorpe, they are plotted within a three-dimensional 'social space'. The first dimension of this space, running along a vertical axis, is the total amount of capital that individuals hold in all three forms – the more you have, the higher you go. Second, and importantly, people are pulled out along a horizontal axis according to the *composition* of their capital stocks – in other words whether it is predominantly economic (as is the case for large industrialists, business owners, financiers, managers and so on), pulling people further right in social space, or cultural (such as for lecturers, teachers, artists), pulling them further left. Social capital is less important in this respect – which is not to say it cannot be as important, just that it is not for Western capitalist societies, and in fact Bourdieu (1998) postulated that in state socialist societies, where economic capital was less significant, social capital, particularly in the form of political connections, was the key principle of differentiation alongside cultural capital. In any case this second axis serves to distinguish further those who would otherwise be lumped together in the same class for Goldthorpe on the basis of a difference in the primary resource at their disposal. The third dimension, or axis, is actually time, or what Bourdieu calls 'trajectory', building into the definition of class the movements of individuals and clusters of individuals over time with social mobility, or if certain jobs start to pay less (returning less economic capital) or begin to require more cultural capital to get into and so on. The resulting model is presented in figure 4.1.

Occupations are used as good proxy measures for position because they demand and perpetuate capital, but they are not

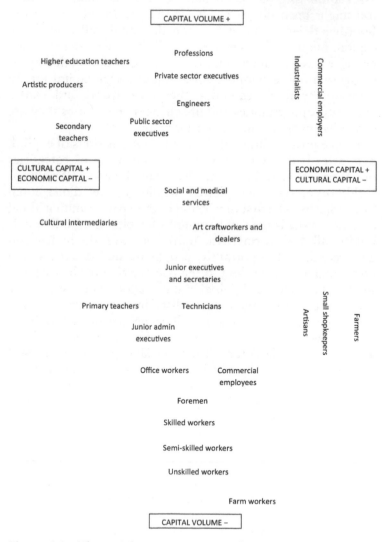

Figure 4.1 The social space in 1960s and 1970s France (based on Bourdieu, 1980: 256–7; 1984: 128–9)

the sole determinants. Unlike for Goldthorpe and Wright, therefore, for Bourdieu people not in work are positioned in the class structure and we can approximate their location so long as we have some information on their capital stocks. Moreover, the position of occupational labels should be understood as central points of areas of dispersion rather than definite locations – an individual teacher with a particular trajectory may actually be positioned more towards the right-hand side of social space, but nevertheless the typical or average position of teachers is in the left-hand side of the dominant class. Unlike the EGP scheme, therefore, Bourdieu's model makes space for the internal heterogeneity of class fractions – indeed, as will be seen a little later, it becomes central to Bourdieu's broader understanding of how class domination and class struggle work. Finally, notice that there are no hard and fast boundaries within the social space between classes. Classes and their internal fractions, said Bourdieu (especially 1987), are best understood as clusters or 'clouds' of individuals similar enough in terms of their key properties to be taken together for analytical purposes, but no one should be misled into thinking that these analytical classes or 'classes on paper' are automatically unified, clearly perceived and identified with or mobilized for action in any way.

Class habitus and symbolic space

Those in similar positions within the social space, with similar levels and types of capital, share similar conditions of existence. By this Bourdieu generally means that position in social space determines one's relative distance from material necessity and all the experiences that go with that. Those in the upper regions of social space, possessing plentiful stocks of capital – whom Bourdieu referred to as the dominant class – are subject to an overall distance from necessity, whilst those in the lower sections with less capital – the dominated class – are somewhat closer to its demands and urgencies. Paying bills, earning money and feeding and clothing oneself are more difficult given low resources and demand more attention.

These differences in conditions of existence, in turn, produce different *habitus*. This is Bourdieu's famous term for every person's complex of durable dispositions, propensities or inclinations to do certain things, our tastes and our likes, but most fundamentally it is how we see, appreciate and value things, all ultimately manifesting in lifestyles and making us who we are. Our habitus is produced through practical adaptation to the situations and the probabilities that come with certain conditions of existence – Bourdieu often refers to this as making a 'virtue of necessity', grounded in the fact that human beings turn what they have into what they want in an effort to attain recognition.

So his masterwork *Distinction* (1984) documents how, on the one hand, the dominant class's distance from necessity grants them time, space and freedom from the practicalities of life to be playful and emphasize 'form over function', 'manner over matter' or 'style over substance', from their choice of food or clothes to ways of walking and looking at a piece of art. On the other hand the dominated class's experience of the demands and exclusions associated with less capital produces a habitus which gives primacy to substance, practicality and functionality and, therefore, disposes people to make the 'choice of the necessary'. To give an example from the world of food, we see amongst those in the upper section of social space, said Bourdieu, a taste for fish and other small, light, refined meals privileging delicate, exquisite taste and presentation, all the product of being removed from the practicalities of feeding oneself and the freedom for creativity and playfulness this allows, versus a taste for hearty, heavy meals with big cuts of meat, potatoes or even fast food among the dominated because these are cheap, substantial, tasty and nourishing and therefore fulfil the function of feeding oneself (and one's family) cheaply.

All these different practices and lifestyles generated by the different class habitus can be superimposed on top of the social space in a space of their own, which Bourdieu called the 'space of lifestyles' (figure 4.2). Here he is trying to overcome Weber's distinction between class and status, because if all these lifestyle practices, goods and activities correspond to positions in social space – or are homologous, to use his term

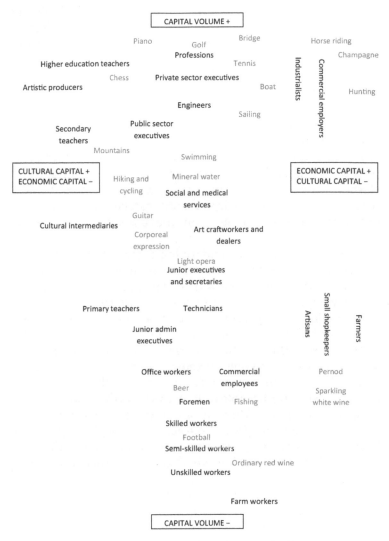

Figure 4.2 The social space (in black) and symbolic space (in grey) in 1960s and 1970s France (based on Bourdieu, 1980: 256–7; 1984: 128–9; 1998: 5)

– then they function as *indicators or symbols of one's class position.* This is why he also called the space of lifestyles the 'symbolic space'. To take a clear example: if you see someone lounging on a private yacht or driving a flashy car, they are statistically most likely to be from the economically dominant section of social space because their conditions of existence are conducive to it, and because of that when we see this lifestyle practice we read it as a sign of this position, of being high in economic capital, but not necessarily in education. This is generally done in relation to our sense of our own position: we see them and make a snap judgement of their position relative to us – as being higher, lower, more or less 'intelligent' or 'cultured', being closer or further away and so on. Bourdieu calls this 'class sense', and though other practices are perhaps less clear cut and give rise to all sorts of clashing categorizations and strategies of self-presentation, they follow the same logic – we still categorize people without even thinking about it on the basis of what we see or hear.

Obviously there is an underlying pattern here – practices and goods based on the taste for form, manner and style correspond to the upper regions of social space, bisected according to whether it takes the *hedonistic, lavish* form of those with predominantly economic capital (luxury cars, boats, expensive holidays) or the *ascetic*, anti-hedonistic, self-cultivating form of those with primarily cultural capital (going to art galleries or museums, listening to classical music etc.), whilst the practices and goods associated with the 'choice of the necessary' are homologous with the lower end. Between these two extremes there is an intermediate class, which Bourdieu called the petite bourgeoisie (though they do not have to be small property owners – he just found the term fitting). They display a lifestyle that betrays their position in the middle, as they aspire to the dominant style of life and distance themselves from the dominated, but have insufficient means and dispositions to consume it in the way deemed legitimate – listening to well-known snippets and sections of operas or symphonies on a 'best of classical music' album rather than the whole works, for example. However, Bourdieu warns us not to fall into the trap of thinking that these practices are *intrinsically* linked to the classes, as if they defined the essence or substance of the classes, because practices can be appropriated and given different meanings, and therefore value, by different classes at different times. The classic example is boxing, which began as a gentlemanly pursuit embodying virtue and honour but which, over time, became more closely associated with the dominated class and its focus on physical strength and ability.

Crucially, these practices are not considered 'different but equal'. Instead, the practices of the dominant are generally presented as exclusive or 'distinguished' whereas those of the dominated are perceived as common and 'vulgar'. This is not because they are *inherently* superior or inferior, but because the dominant possess the power, through the media, schools and politics, to impose their way of life as the legitimate one. Education, high culture, financial success, lavish lifestyles – these are all seen as 'good things' to which people should aspire, but in actual fact only derive their meaning in relation to that which is perceived as their opposite: the common, the widespread, popular culture and so on. The lifestyle of the dominated serves as a kind of 'negative foil' against which the dominant define themselves and the legitimate ways of being, and the dominated for the most part know the dominant lifestyle is generally considered better than theirs. There may be resistance and struggle, they may well value and rationalize their own way of doing things, but they still recognize – or rather *misrecognize*, since it is arbitrary – that, overall, the activities of others are defined as more legitimate or worthy and what one needs to do to 'get ahead'. All this – being compelled to see one's life and lifestyle through the denigrating lens of someone else's – Bourdieu refers to as 'symbolic violence'.

The evolution of cultural domination?

One immediate reaction to Bourdieu's theory of social space and symbolic space so far might be to hark back to the ideas mentioned in chapter 1 on postmodernism. Surely lifestyles nowadays are no longer moored in social structures but reflexively and playfully put together by self-creating individuals? Surely the boundaries between the 'high culture' of those in the upper regions of social space and the popular culture of the working class have collapsed and left behind nothing but transient subcultures – Goths, skaters, emos, hipsters etc. (Pakulski and Waters, 1996)? In actual fact this is a theme Bourdieu spotted when he was writing *Distinction*, and he not only disproved it empirically but turned the argument upside down. What he found was that a new cluster was emerging in the culturally rich middle sections of social space made up of individuals in the media and educational industries downwardly mobile from the dominant class. In an effort to compensate for or suppress their descent this 'new petite bourgeoisie' developed a lifestyle oriented around trying to avoid being pinned down in social space by others, or a 'dream of social flying' as Bourdieu put it – rejecting established cultural hierarchies, valorizing self-realization, playfulness, variety and so on. Not only that, but they also tried to propagate this as the legitimate way to live through their jobs in media, education, politics and so on. Far from signalling the end of class, therefore, postmodern culture was in fact the *product* of class. This theme was taken up by Featherstone (1991) and Lash (1990), but unfortunately many sociologists were taken in by the propagation attempt and started trying to give it lofty theoretical status.

More recently there has been another development. Maybe postmodernists went too far in rejecting *any* correspondence between class and lifestyles, argue some, but that does not mean cultural domination across Western nations today (let alone others) is precisely as Bourdieu found in 1960s and 1970s France. Actually, argue many, if we look at survey data across contemporary Europe and North America, what we find is that the major class divide is not between highbrow 'snobs' and the lowbrow popular masses, but between affluent, cosmopolitan 'omnivores' who consume a bit of everything in true postmodern style – popular music and classical music, independent films and Hollywood blockbusters – and a dominated class who tend to stick to only one or two types of music, film or whatever (Peterson, 1992). In other words, cultural domination is about breadth of tastes versus narrow tastes, and the underpinning disposition of the former is often said to hinge on worldly openness and tolerance rather than symbolic mastery or economic capital.

After a period of considerable prominence, however, some telling limitations of the research underpinning this thesis started to emerge, such as its reliance on 'catch-all' genre categories, its inability to pick up aesthetic dispositions rather than just which music, TV programmes and so on one thinks one likes, and the use of measures of class at odds with Bourdieu's own (see especially Holt, 1997; Atkinson, 2011a). More interestingly, at about the same time, there emerged a cluster of studies in Scandinavia following Bourdieu's own method and logic much more closely and finding distinct continuities (e.g. Prieur et al., 2008; Rosenlund, 2009). The precise practices and goods making up the national symbolic space may be different, but the underpinning patterns of difference and the aesthetic dispositions underlying them seemed more or less stable. Some debate has since been sparked, however, by a massive (and controversial) study of the British class structure undertaken in a broadly Bourdieu-sian spirit by Savage et al. (2013). While recognizing that forms of 'high culture' still reflect cultural capital in the contemporary UK, this team argue that they do so mainly among the old, while among the young it may be more symbolically valuable to play video games or attend gigs. The methodological shortcomings of this research, however, invite caution in taking too seriously its claims (Atkinson and Rosenlund, 2014).

Class-making

So far we have documented the existence of 'analytical classes' or 'classes on paper', that is, classes of people clustered in the social and symbolic spaces on the basis of similar conditions of existence, habitus and lifestyle practices which can be separated out for research purposes. There are no rigid boundaries or definite criteria of membership, and there is no assumption of solidarity, collectivism or belonging to some particular 'group' with a name (the 'working class') beyond the general sense of similarity and difference. Yet people within media, political and academic discourse constantly talk about and discuss and debate the existence of 'classes', of distinct groups with names and interests and boundaries and criteria – having X makes you 'working class', doing Y makes you 'middle class' and so on. Bourdieu argued this is the nature of human perception: we carve up the world into categories and groups, name them and associate them with things, oppose them to other categories, define their features, gather with people we consider to be in the same category as us and sometimes even represent them and fight for them against others, as with trade unions representing the 'working class'. So people divide up the social space in perception – not necessarily coherently by any means – through associating certain symbols with certain names through experience. This can take the form of the explicit discourse of 'classes', but it can also work through similar terms which do exactly the same job of representing a section of social space and symbolic space, including that which one sees oneself as in – toffs, the posh, the rich, scum, underclass, 'chav', bourgeoisie and proletariat (i.e. Marx himself was part of this process) and so on (for the most detailed examination of this process, see Boltanski, 1987).

Of course some people's categorizations of the social world stick more than others and have more general purchase. This is based on two things: first, the degree to which the categories are anchored in the actual differences of social space – the idea that a distinguishable 'class' exists that stretches over random areas of social space is unlikely to garner credibility – and, second, the power of the person doing the labelling, i.e. the degree to which they are (mis)recognized as an 'authority', or as someone who 'knows what they are talking about', and given a platform in the media or politics. Hence dominant categories of thought often win out, and Bourdieu called this power to impose one's own worldview as common sense *symbolic power*. None of these representations of social space refer to actually existing groups, however. There are no substantial criteria of membership in reality – all that exists is the social space and the symbolic space and the words we use to describe them (Bourdieu, 1998: 12), even if representations and their representatives can have real effects on the distributions within social space, such as tightening up or altering the position of certain clusters through, for example, increased credentialization or better remuneration.

The field of power

At several points the ability of those rich in capital to make their judgements and labels stick, to make them generally taken for granted – or, to use a favourite term of Bourdieu's, *doxic* – and to propagate them using the media, politics, education and so on has cropped up. To finish this run-through of Bourdieu's perspective, then, let me elaborate how he conceives of this in a little more detail, not only because many commentators neglect it but because it serves as another key point of difference from other schools of thought. For whilst most Marxists (not all, but most) would see the process in terms of a relatively unified bourgeoisie controlling the state and its institutions, and Weberians would see it in terms of party or, with John Scott, in terms of elites, what exists at the top of the class structure for Bourdieu is a 'field of power'. The first step of the argument here, returning to the earlier point on internal heterogeneity of class fractions, is that individuals contend not just within the social space for recognition but within all manner of 'fields' such as politics, the media, religion, art, literature, journalism, science, law and business, each with its own specific forms of capital, its own internal struggles and conflicts and its own dominant and dominated groupings. Some Marxists might have no problem recognizing these fields as specific 'apparatuses' of domination (Althusser, 1971), but while they might identify internal 'contradictions' within them they still tend to portray them as fairly homogeneous or abstract structures devoid of actual people, whereas for Bourdieu they are universes of difference and contention defined by the struggles and strategies of flesh-and-blood individuals to win the forms of recognition in their particular field, with very complex effects on the external world.

Second, many of these particular fields exist within a meta-field of struggle called the field of power. Here the key players in those different fields struggle against one another to impose the authority and definitions of reality that have currency in their fields as the overall dominant one in society. The main struggle here is between the possessors of power in the field of business, or economic production – industrialists, magnates, bankers, financiers, press barons – versus the possessors of power in the fields of cultural production – intellectuals, educators, artists, writers – and Bourdieu was clear that the economic fraction of the dominant class, those in the economic field, were winning in this regard. Hence they were the 'dominant fraction of the dominant class', and money the dominant measure of all things, whereas intellectuals and so on are the 'dominated fraction of the dominant class'. As to the fields of ideological production in between (politics, media, law), which do most to transmit the views and language of these fractions to the population, they are torn between the two sides, with different people in them representing the interests of each – manifesting in divides between left wing and right wing, for example.

Four ripostes from the old guard and some responses

Many see Bourdieu's ideas as successfully reinvigorating the study of class, but there are others who are less pleased with his current popularity. Critics of particular aspects of his work we will see in future chapters, but on a general level there have been considerable rumbles of dissatisfaction from the 'old guard' in class analysis, i.e. those advocating, or even just sympathetic to, Marxist and Weberian approaches. Four points of criticism can be singled out in particular, but I believe four responses, drawing on the logic of Bourdieu's theory if not necessarily the letter, can be fired right back.

First, Weberians such as Chan and Goldthorpe (2010) have objected to Bourdieu's claim that he was overcoming Weber's separation of class and status by theorizing the homology of social space and symbolic space. Statistical data, so they argue, proves cultural practices have no relationship to class whatsoever but are associated with status groups, as Chan and Goldthorpe define and operationalize them in research, thus proving that class and status are analytically separable. One should be wary of such claims, however, since Chan and Goldthorpe are basing this on their own narrow definition of class, which excludes cultural capital and the second axis of social space from the picture. If we include education in any analysis, as cultural capital, then we find, as Chan and Goldthorpe themselves admit, that there is a strong impact on lifestyles, but they steadfastly refuse to see this as part and parcel of class.

Second, some claim that all the focus on cultural processes, the symbolic dimension of class and lifestyles risks sidelining the *economic* dimension of class – i.e. inequalities of wealth, opportunities and life chances, the poisonous practices of big business, market and productive relations and so on – which all, of course, remain important (Crompton and Scott, 2005; Sayer, 2005; Flemmen, 2013). However, it should be remembered that economic capital is a crucial factor in distributing people in social space, a fundamental source of misrecognition in capitalist societies and therefore constitutive of conditions of existence, and that the dynamics of the economic field within the field of power – wherein employment and market relations are shaped and struggled over as part of the more general quest for recognition – are fundamental for understanding contemporary societies. So it is not that those inspired by Bourdieu are *unable* to look at economic inequalities and domination, only that they have tended not to focus on them so much (yet) because they are still exploring modes of cultural domination.

Third, Bourdieu has often been described as a 'pessimist' because resistance and challenge to the status quo are supposedly impossible. Related to this, the cultural class analysts themselves, as well as former colleagues of Bourdieu, have expressed some reservation over Bourdieu's treatment of the dominated class: if they are defined by *lack* of capital, whether economic, cultural, social or symbolic, how do we make sense of how they draw value and possess their own autonomous sources of power and recognition – their sociability, their humour, their own cultural practices (Passeron and Grignon, 1989; Savage, 2000; Skeggs, 2011; Bennett et al., 2009)? The clearest contrast here is perhaps with the Gramscian CCCS, which saw youth subcultures among the working class as forms of symbolic resistance against capitalist domination.

The immediate response is twofold. On the one hand, the social and symbolic spaces are always seen as fields of struggle, so there is bound to be resistance from the most

dominated and efforts to subvert the worldview of the dominant by asserting other ways of being, even other sources of
recognition, as legitimate, albeit – and we should be realistic
here, as was Bourdieu's tendency – with difficulty and limited
success. Bourdieu is not really so different from Gramsci here,
except that there is a clearer account of where cultural styles
come from and the model of the genesis of doxa is considerably more nuanced than the model of the imposition of
hegemony. On the other hand, while the social space is meant
to represent a general balance sheet of symbolic power on the
national scale, if we want the full picture we have to take into
account the multiple, smaller-scale and often localized fields
in which people can be placed and in which they contend for
the forms of recognition valued there. They may well be
outside the field of power, and they may therefore be of little
consequence for the production and distribution of *general-
ized* definitions of what is 'legitimate', but they nevertheless
form relatively autonomous microcosms in which worth and
symbolic power are sought and won by people of all positions
in the social space. This certainly seems to be the direction in
which Bourdieu was going in his later work – indeed a pro-
jected but uncompleted work was to be called *Microcosms*.
The family is just one example we will return to at a later
point, and other researchers have begun to examine fields of
particular popular or middlebrow cultural practices, such as
amateur wind bands (Dubois et al., 2013); but an illustration
I want to pursue a bit further, pieced together from a few
Bourdieu-inspired studies, is the struggle over *physical capital*
within *local social spaces*.

Physical capital is a concept mentioned rarely by Bourdieu
(e.g. 1990b: 122), though it has been developed a little by
Wacquant (1995, 2004) in his study of boxing. In its most
general form it refers to the capital of fighting strength, physical force and martial skill. It is, quite simply, the domination
of others, or the gaining of 'respect' or *recognition* in some
way, through perceived capacity to overpower others physically by hand or weapon. It can be developed and accumulated through investment of other resources (gym membership,
weapons etc.), but that is hardly necessary – physical capital,
as an elementary form of domination, is to some degree
bounded by the capacities of the body given at birth but, in

principle, cultivatable with few material or cultural resources, even if, as Shilling (2003) rightly points out, they can be transient and fragile sources of power for that. Physical capital is not gender-specific by definition, but has, historically, tended to be (mostly) monopolized by men and thus bound up with particular notions of masculinity (cf. Connell, 2005). Hence possession of physical capital, whether by males or females, is often associated in everyday perception with being 'manly', while its lack is construed as 'feminine'.

Since physical capital is a relatively accessible form of power attainable through practical, bodily mastery, many of those who face difficulty attaining the 'legitimate' modes of recognition (i.e. cultural or economic capital) turn to it as either a means of achieving other forms of recognition or a source of recognition in its own right. They make a virtue of necessity, in other words, and turn what they can have into what they value: 'hardness', 'toughness', 'being a man' and so on. Given the distribution of symbolic power within society, however, physical prowess has limited exchangeability – it is not, in other words, a symbolic capital within *national* social spaces – and can only be plied in specific fields, namely either those sanctioned by the holders of 'legitimate' power because it aligns with commercial or state interests, such as sports, military and security services and so on, or *local* social spaces in the form of a reputation for being 'hard' or 'tough'.

A 'local social space' refers to the distribution of recognition and power within a certain community or neighbourhood, where networks are dense and mutual awareness fairly high – a class system in micro, essentially, based on local forms of value. A village might be one example (Bourdieu, 1999a: 127–8n), but research frequently shows that deprived urban areas, such as Harlem in New York (Bourgois, 2003), housing projects on Chicago's South Side (Wacquant, 1999) or St Ann's estate in Nottingham (McKenzie, 2012), tend to operate like this, perhaps because of the limits placed on geographical mobility by intergenerational poverty (see also Nayak, 2006; France et al., 2012). In these cases the local social spaces act as microcosms in which, notwithstanding the general acceptance of the legitimacy of economic capital, the struggles against the usual sources of recognition are played out, *but between fractions of the dominated class*, i.e. those trying to 'get on' and accumulate cultural capital at one pole versus those imposing, amongst other things (street style, mastery of slang, street 'smarts', hustling etc.), 'toughness' and 'hardness' as legitimate at the other, with many muddling in between. So the dominated class are not completely power-less – they are not, as Bourdieu's critics lament, entirely exempt from or in every situation losers in the constant strug-gle for recognition that underpins human existence. Yet while physical capital does, in its way, represent resistance against the doxa peddled by the powerful, the irony is that it is not the dominant or even the intermediate class with whom they struggle and against whom they most often deploy their resources, but the other fractions of the working class within their local social space.

This extension of Bourdieu's theory can also help dissolve the final criticism sometimes aimed at it: that it represents a rather ahistorical vision of classes, i.e. one that not only has little to say about, but may even be unable to grasp, the emergence, change and evolution of class structures from feudalism (and before) to capitalism – bread and butter for many Marxists and Weberians (Calhoun, 1993; Gartman, 1991; Hobsbawm, 2007). This is because physical capital has played nothing less than a pivotal role in Western history. It has, after all, been a primary source of (male) recognition and power since the earliest civilizations, from Mesopotamia to ancient Greece, and took centre stage in Europe following the collapse of the Roman Empire and the emergence of multiple kingdoms as warlords converted their military supremacy into a basic form of economic capital – with associated signs, such as jewellery, adding another layer of recognition – by extracting, on pain of death or assault, payment (usually called 'tribute') from people trying their best to farm the land for survival.

As the warlord – taking the title of 'king' or some equiva-lent – parcelled his land out to his soldiers (knights and vassals), and they in turn began to struggle for favour, for independence or even to usurp the throne (remember the overview of feudalism in chapter 1), they inevitably formed a field of their own, stretching over a certain territory and opposed to the religious field comprising all the priests, abbots and monks of the land. Such was the feudal field of power. In the process, as painstakingly chronicled by Elias (2000), physical capital then slowly underwent a progressive *delegitimization*. The royal (or knightly/aristocratic) field evolved into a 'court society' in which recognition and domination through the symbolic capital of honour, loyalty and 'good behaviour', i.e. through *symbolic* violence, began to take primacy. Physical violence, its opposite, was thus necessarily denigrated as 'barbaric' except in specific legitimated and regulated forms, such as the military or sports. In other words, physical capital was losing its role as a symbolic capital in the field of power, instead being valued only in increasingly restricted domains. Bourdieu himself then picks up the story to trace two developments: (1) the subsequent emergence, via the church, of cultural capital in the place of courtly symbolic capital in the West with the growth of education alongside economic capital, the latter having also begun to increase in importance through the steady commodification of land, labour and goods (Bourdieu, 2004a); and (2) the knitting together of the medieval patchwork of local social spaces (manors, towns, villages) overseen by the feudal field of power into national social spaces through the integration of local goods and labour markets and state-building enabled by communications, transport developments and so on (Bourdieu, 2008, 2014), though evidently with certain locales still acting as subfields of the national balance of power where physical capital can thrive. All in all, the history of all hitherto existing society can perhaps be rewritten as a history of the struggle for recognition and the imposition by some on others of certain arbitrary principles of recognition which they possess – physical strength, nobility, religious virtue, money or intelligence – as the dominant ones: they become the people looked up to and valued in a society in one way or another, though only for so long.

Conclusion

Thus concludes our tour of the three key perspectives in class analysis today. As we have seen, the turn towards Bourdieu in recent years has been part of the 'cultural turn' in sociology more generally, as this French thinker could allow researchers to emphasize aspects of class which the prevailing approaches had neglected and solve problems they had run into. Many instances of this will be encountered over subsequent chapters. It must be stressed, however, that Bourdieu offers much more than has generally been taken on by 'cultural class analysts' hitherto – he is useful not only for understanding differences in lifestyle, identities and educational performance, for which his concepts have been put to most frequent use. Tools are also there for opening up the nature and evolution of economic domination and inequality; the varied forms of resistance and alternative forms of recognition available; the emergence and vicissitudes of all sorts of 'groups' or 'subcultures' with apparently shared interests, values and identities; and the historical transformation of structures of socio-cultural difference as certain modes of recognition come to prominence and compete to different degrees with others. Bourdieu can thus accommodate many Marxist and Weberian interests, from the genesis of exploitation to the patterning of life chances, but within an overarching framework that often requires they be turned on their heads.

5
Intersections

However class might be defined – whether in terms of exploitation, life chances or misrecognition – there is the tricky issue
of how it relates to other forms of inequality and difference.
For a long time in the twentieth century the question was
barely raised, let alone explored at length. Class, in one form
or another, was simply seen as the most important division,
and economic exploitation, industrial strife and communism
versus liberalism the most pressing issues of the day – all else
were epiphenomena of little overall significance. From about
the 1960s onwards, however, social science in general started
to come under fire from two directions, largely because of
particular social changes in the West, and the sociology of
class was certainly no exception. The first direction was feminism, which grew in force following the increased participation of women in higher education and the workforce, a trend
spurred by the steady shift towards a service- and knowledge-
based economy as well as advances in contraceptive technology. The second was a line of argument highlighting the
blindness of sociology and other disciplines to ethnic or racial
differences, and indeed to their own 'Eurocentric' bias, this
time sparked by the waves of migration to Europe from
former colonies in the post-war period or increased access to
higher education among dominated ethnic groups in the US.
There have since been other voices articulating the importance
of, for example, age, generation, sexuality and disability too,

but these two particular fonts of criticism have troubled sociologists, including researchers of class, the longest and the
most. What I want to do in this chapter, then, is examine
these two lines of attack, how they challenged class analysis,
how the different traditions of class research have responded
by trying to theorize the links and how successful they appear
to have been, all with the ultimate intention of clarifying
where class analysis currently stands. We can start with
gender for no other reason than its impact on mainstream
class research was felt slightly earlier and more intensely.

The feminist critique

Class, in the Marxist and Weberian versions prevalent through
much of the last century, is essentially about the world of paid
work, whether because of its implication in the production
process or because of the life chances it affords, and the
institutions of the public sphere – the state, law, religion –
which sustain it. All of these, highlighted feminists, are popu-
lated overwhelmingly by men and have little bearing on the
experiences of most women, who, despite their amplified
education and labour market participation, are still tied to
the private, domestic sphere (through childrearing, house-
work etc.) in a way men simply are not. To focus on class
alone is therefore to focus only on roughly half the population, to look at squabbles largely between men and to ignore
completely not only the subjugation of women – the violence
they suffer at the hands of men, their confinement to the
home, discrimination in the workplace and so on, all symp-
tomatic of a *patriarchal* power structure – but how that
subjugation might itself sustain the system as a whole (see
e.g. Delphy, 1984).

More profoundly, argued some, the very concept of class
and the methodology of class researchers are inherently gen-
der-blind. This was nowhere made clearer than in the long
and heated debate which took place between Goldthorpe,
feminists and others in the 1980s over the 'unit of analysis'
in class research, i.e. what or who one should gather information about in any piece of research and assign a class to. Is

it, in other words, the individual who has a class position, or the family as a whole? This debate was sparked by Goldthorpe (1983), who wrote a paper, in response to earlier feminist critics (e.g. Acker, 1973), defending what he called the 'conventional view': the idea that the unit of analysis in class research should be the household, that the head of the household should stand for the class position of the household as a whole, and that it just happens – such is the nature of patriarchy in Western societies – that the head of the household is usually male. The result is that we take the man's occupation and his answers to whatever survey questions as definitive no matter what the wife does for a living or what she thinks – she's categorized as belonging to the same class as her husband and having the same view. For example, even if a woman is in a prestigious profession such as medicine, but works part time because she is also expected to look after the family and therefore earns less, and the husband is a relatively well-paid skilled manual worker, they are both classed as manual workers and slotted into one of the working-class categories.

This, argued a collection of critics, is absurd (Heath and Britten, 1984; Stanworth, 1984; Marshall et al., 1988). Especially with the increased participation of women in the workforce, including top-level professions and positions of authority, and their increased educational success, the idea that their employment is secondary to that of their husbands, and that they are considered unimportant just because they perhaps work fewer hours or are paid less because of the gender gap in pay, is not only analytically deficient but a little sexist. It ignores, for one thing, the existence and importance of what are called *cross-class families*, where the husband and wife occupy very different positions in the class structure and therefore surely have divergent views and attitudes (see e.g. McRae, 1988). It also presupposes that women's employment is secondary to their family commitments and that they somehow absorb their husband's values and views no matter what job they are in themselves – the best predictor of their views is, in other words, not their own occupation but their husband's.

A lot of this criticism also highlighted the fact that men and women have very different relations to the labour market.

If we look at the distribution of men and women within Goldthorpe's classes, it becomes apparent that women are crowded into the middle section, the 'intermediate class' of low-level non-manual work or personal service work: typists, secretaries, office workers, catering, childcare and the like. Not only that, but being in this class has radically different meanings for men and women: for men, it is often a stepping stone early in their working lives to mobility up the career ladder and the class hierarchy, whereas for women it is usually a dead-end, lifelong job. So classes and fractions of classes are *gendered*, and this distorts the statistical pattern of life chances between the different classes – suddenly we have very little social mobility in one class compared to others. But class analysis is unable to recognize this because it refuses to recognize the idea that women have a *different employment relationship* from men because they are oppressed, or more specifically because they are filtered into certain occupations on the basis of socially produced expectations of what women can and should do, and are prevented from movement by the constraining expectations of family commitments and, of course, sex discrimination.

Goldthorpe (1987) has actually yielded to some, though not all, of these criticisms, examining the social mobility of women and even modifying his scheme a little, essentially dividing class III (routine non-manual workers) into two parts – one for men, one for women – and when class outcomes for women are in focus this feminized class category is treated as working class rather than intermediate class in recognition of the fact that it is essentially governed by a labour contract and furnishes equivalent life chances. His colleague Robert Erikson (1984) also proposed that researchers should always try to take the 'dominant' person in the household as the proxy for the household's class position by actually determining who the family breadwinner is in all cases – male or female – and singling them out for analysis. This seems to have closed the case so far as the Nuffield School are concerned, but it hardly won leagues of feminist fans. The fact is, it would not really have mattered what Goldthorpe said – feminists were not particularly interested in a neo-Weberian approach to class anyway. They either wanted to jettison the concept of economic class altogether – or, more accurately, to see gender as the real basis of what we might call 'class' divisions within society, as was the case for the declining number of radical feminists such as Millett (1971) and Firestone (1970) – or, more likely, sought to understand the ways in which gender domination co-exists with class domination, but in terms of the prevalent paradigm of radical political critique around at the time: Marxism.

Marxism and feminism: from an unhappy marriage to mariticide

The union of Marxism and feminism has been tempestuous to say the least, the main source of strife being the extent to which patriarchy is seen as autonomous from productive relations. Some took the classic 'Marxist-feminist' stance, derived from Friedrich Engels' (1990) work on the origin of the family, private property and the state, in which patriarchy is essentially reducible to economic relations. Engels himself tied the origin of patriarchy to the prehistoric domestication of animals, the first private means of production, which were technically owned and controlled by men and then passed on from father to son. With the exclusion of women from owner-ship and control they were not only relegated to the home but treated as secondary within the home – the master of property became the master of the house – and eventually this consolidated into the bourgeois nuclear family model. Only with the abolition of private property will we get the abolition of oppression within the family and truly free monogamous 'sex-love', as Engels called it. Seccombe (1974) added to this historical sketch that women's domestic labour today – childcare and so on – is an important element of capitalist relations of production in so far as it reproduces the labour power of men (by nourishing them and bringing up the next generation of workers) and facilitates the inter-nalization of ideology (through the ideas women impart to their children).

Others were rather less happy about this economic deter-minism, which seemed to represent a decidedly one-sided and miserable 'marriage' of feminism and Marxism since the latter essentially subsumed the former (Hartmann, 1979), and so they strove to find ways of conceiving patriarchy as a more or less independent principle of domination. Delphy (1984), for example, made the case that the domestic division of labour should be seen as a mode of production unto itself, distinct from the capitalist mode of production, in which men exploit women by appropriating the fruits of their labour (i.e. having their meals cooked for them, their shirts ironed and so on) with minimal monetary maintenance. Barrett (1980), on the other hand, criticized Delphy and others for keeping gender oppression and capitalism *too* separate and instead tried to ride the wave of structural Marxism (much like Poulantzas) to argue that gender domination, being largely ideological in character, is only *relatively* autonomous from material relations. Drawing on Gardiner (1977), she also made the case that women have a *dual relationship* to class: on the one hand, through the direct exploitation of their own labour power in paid employment, which became increasingly important in the later twentieth century, but also, on the other hand, as mediated by their dependence on a husband's wage which is itself the product of exploitation.

This distinction between direct and mediated relationships to class relations was later taken up by Wright (1997), who wanted to know which were more important for actually shaping the views, values and votes of women. In fact, he concluded, it tends to depend on the national context. For example, in the US it does appear that women's class identities and interests are shaped more by their husband's class position than their own, but this is not the case for Sweden. Wright does, however, claim that there may be very good *material* reasons for this – for example, the more generous welfare state in Sweden means women are less dependent on men materially, and in Sweden class identity is linked more to unions and workplace experience, whereas in the US community and consumption are more important.

Eventually, however, the strained union of Marxism and feminism more or less fell to pieces. Sure enough, increasingly influential voices heralding the need for 'intersectional' analysis, in which gender, class and race are all depicted as mutually interpenetrating, still tended to rely in some way on a vaguely Marxist understanding of class relations (e.g. Collins, 2001), but the most influential strands of feminist theory per se turned away from class altogether. This is in good part because a lot of feminism in the 1980s and into the 1990s was part of the cultural turn, which we have already seen, and was in fact central to the associated journey in social theory from Marxism through structural Marxism, in which ideology was given room for autonomous manoeuvre, to poststructuralism, especially as represented by Michel Foucault, in which discourses unattached to any social location take primacy. Judith Butler's (1990) work on the ways in which gender identity is performed from situation to situation, repeatedly enacting dominant discourses about what gendered behaviour does and should involve and perpetuating the illusion of a universal male or female nature, is perhaps the clearest landmark in this shift of emphasis. The conversion of Michele Barrett (1991), however, is probably the most telling: once a defender of a materialist feminism, even if suitably critical of Marx, she eventually decided his economic reductionism and determinism were too much to stomach and championed the post-Marxist turn instead.

Not all feminists went so far, though. Many were sympathetic to the new emphasis on the way in which identity and being are bound up with struggles to define the world and recognized the problems of Marxism, but refused to do away with the concept of class as an analytical tool altogether. Quite the contrary: only by bringing in class is it possible to identify the interests underpinning certain discourses and definitions of the world, not so much in terms of deceiving the dominated so as to continue extracting surplus value, but in terms of people seeking to promote their own ways of life, grounded in possession of multiple resources, as legitimate by denigrating others. If that sounds a bit like Bourdieu's approach to class, that is no coincidence: the impulse to reconnect culture to class in feminist theory drew many to the Frenchman's ideas and, indeed, was fundamental to their popularization. Having said that, Bourdieu's take on gender and its intersection with class has hardly been uncritically accepted, nor, to be frank, has it always been particularly well understood.

Bourdieu and feminism: a happier marriage?

The starting point seems all well and good. For one thing, Bourdieu's definition of class manages to avoid many of the issues which turned feminists away from the Nuffield approach. It sidesteps the whole debate over the unit of analysis and the neglect of women, for example, by assuming that it is *individuals* that are plotted in social space, not households, whether or not they have a job, but that we can make sense of the experiences and dispositions of homemakers and couples (married or not, cohabiting or not) by factoring in social capital, the capital by proxy, i.e. the advantages and resources one has in life because of association with certain others (Atkinson, 2009). One partner in the relationship may be a typist and the other a lawyer, but each, through the link of social capital, feeds off the capital of the other, shaping their individual position in social space, their conditions of existence and hence their habitus. Of course this is not an automatic process – sometimes access of one partner to the capital of the other may be strictly controlled or dependent on the power relations within the family itself, and that has to be factored into the equation.

However, Bourdieu's explicit position on gender as it was presented in *Distinction* was criticized by some on the basis that he, like Marxism, seemed to treat it as secondary to class (Anthias, 2001; Adkins and Skeggs, 2004). The impression given is that, causally, the impact of gender on habitus depends on location in social space, not vice versa, and in fact gendered differences in habitus tend to reduce, he said, the higher up and further towards the cultural pole in social space one goes – women start reading the same newspapers, playing the same sports and liking the same plays, for example, as men – meaning class dictates the style and extent of gender dispositions. Also, if we remember the argument on the formation of perceptual categories such as 'the working class' and their grounding in the objective divisions of the social space, the implication is that any attempt to rally women together as a group like this will always be dashed by the class differences which run through them.

Bourdieu's position on gender was, however, later refined in his little book on *Masculine Domination* (2001). Here he makes clear that gender domination is in fact the 'paradigmatic form' of domination. The binary division between male and female, a historical product only very loosely based on biology, appears most natural of all divisions and actually transcends class, nations and epochs. Gender is, in other words, considered autonomous from class but intersecting with it in different ways. For example, historically accumulated expectations of what men and women should and can do, transmitted through family, school and the dominant players within the field of power, are embodied, producing a gendered habitus which includes perceptions of what positions and heights of social space and the field of power are attainable and even desirable for women and men. Together with pay differences and sexism, based on the perception of what is 'appropriate' for men and women, including the assumption that women are less committed to the workforce because they value family more, this serves to distribute men and women unevenly within the social space – women tend to cluster in the lower and the cultural-capital-rich sections – and filter them into specific fields at different rates and positions. It also produces affinities between women no matter what their class position, and thus the possibility for mobilization equivalent to efforts at 'class-making'. For all these reasons Bourdieu called gender a 'symbolic coefficient', since it compounds domination in the social space.

Clearly, then, Bourdieu did not see women as somehow 'outside' of the social space, as one often reproduced criticism has it (e.g. Lovell, 2000), and his general approach has been readily taken up by feminists such as Skeggs (1997), Lawler (2000) and Reay (1998) to explore the ways in which class is gendered and gender is classed, with specific categories and pathologizations put forward by those in power, through the media and political debates, of ways of being a woman. There are thus supposedly 'wrong' or inferior ways to be female (loud, raucous, 'vulgar', aggressive) or a mother (uninvolved in their children's education, unable or unwilling to help with schoolwork, overly emotional or confrontational with teachers etc.), all of which are readings of dispositions stemming from conditions of existence in the lower sections of social space. Nevertheless, the general sentiment amongst sympathetic feminists still seems to be that while Bourdieu's conceptualization of class and the social world in general might be very useful, his actual conceptualization of gender per se, even in his later work, is not quite good enough. His binary understanding of gender, for example, is pilloried for homogenizing the experiences of men and women and thus not only missing the complexity of gender differences (androgyny, third genders, transsexualism etc.) but casting women as uniformly dominated, ignoring their resistance and struggle as well as the fact that femininity may act as a resource in some situations (Lovell, 2000; Anthias, 2001; Mottier, 2002; Adkins and Skeggs, 2004; Huppatz, 2012).

The first charge seems somewhat unfair – a binary, understood in fully relational terms, does not exclude difference and diversity but merely underscores that any difference is always defined by its relative position vis-à-vis the two poles of 'masculinity' and 'femininity' understood as doxic categories of perception (cf. Moi, 1991). The issue of struggle and femininity as a resource, on the other hand, is a bit more vexed and has prompted all sorts of attempts to twist and mould Bourdieu's concepts in the hope of finding a solution. Some, for example, have argued that femininity acts as a distinct 'gender capital', either in the social space alongside economic, cultural and social capital, or within specific fields (McCall, 1992; Skeggs, 2004; Huppatz, 2012). Some have posited that there is a 'gender field' in which definitions of masculinity and femininity are struggled over, with dominant and dominated variants, symbolic capital and symbolic violence aplenty and particular points of intersection with class – for example, working-class versions of 'hyper' masculinity or femininity might be denigrated along with homosexuality, androgyny and so on (Coles, 2007). Others have made the case that if not gender per se then perhaps sexual attractiveness, which is evidently gendered, works as a form of capital, again either in the social space (where it can be converted into other capitals) or within specific fields (Hakim, 2012; Green, 2014). Physical capital is relevant here too. What the future holds for these ideas – whether one or the other will prove more productive for research than Bourdieu's own concepts and whether they are fully coherent – is uncertain since they are at fairly early stages of development, but this is an area of growing interest.

Ethno-racial domination and class

Such is the current state of thought on the relationship between class and gender. So what about ethnicity? In fact the general story possesses considerable parallels, though with its own particularities. First, in the wake of the civil rights movement in the US and successive waves of migration from soon-to-be-former colonies into European nations after the Second World War, came the critique. On the one hand, there was the rather fundamental criticism that class theory, like much of sociology, was inherently 'Eurocentric', i.e. it attempted to portray specifically European divisions and struggles as nothing less than the motors of all of world history, grossly reducing all conflict and ways of being to a category and an associated story of human development with significance in only a small part of the globe (Said, 1978; Robinson, 1983; Young, 1990). The target here was usually Marxism, though perhaps ironically many of the early and most famous anti-colonialist thinkers such as Frantz Fanon or C. L. R. James were heavily influenced by Marx.

On the other hand, there was the more substantive argument that class theory of all stripes was failing to make sense of many of the current key clashes and inequalities in the West. Immigration and the development in deprived areas of new communities, whether African-Caribbeans or Asians in the UK, North Africans in France or Turks in Germany and so on, contributed to the fragmentation and weakening of white working-class communities, cultures and identities by creating new tensions and conflicts in the competition for jobs and social housing. Divisions were and continue to be drawn between – to use Elias and Scotson's (1990) terms – 'established' residents and (ethnic) 'outsiders', producing animosity and varying levels of violence, securing a central place for 'race relations' on the political agenda and ultimately, as people such as Ulrich Beck (1992) argue, overtaking or blotting out the focus on inequalities and divisions of class within the white population.

Not only that, but the quickest glance at national statistics will reveal that ethnic minorities are consistently and disproportionately in the lower social positions of society and experience fewer life chances in the Weberian sense, whether in health, education or social mobility, and, importantly, this is not just down to their parents or themselves being in under-privileged class positions because it still seems to stick when education and class position are accounted for. For example, in the UK Modood et al. (1997) found that 40 per cent of white males with A-levels (academic school qualifications) gain work in the service class, using Goldthorpe's terms, whereas only 30 per cent of Indian men and 15 per cent of Caribbean men with exactly the same qualifications do. The figures are similar for women, except that fewer achieve service class status than do men in all categories.

This difference can be attributed in part to prejudice, racism and discrimination based on the prevailing ideas about ethnic groups (Muslims as extremists, black people as lazy, Roma as thieves and such like), especially as they relate to legacies of colonial domination and post-colonialism. But there is also variation between the different ethnic groups as well: the Chinese, for example, do remarkably well in the UK even compared to the white British population, whilst the Bangladeshi and Pakistani communities do particularly badly. Some writers put this down to the cultural traits or values of the different ethnic groups – Modood (2004), for example, has put forward a concept of 'ethnic capital' to explain the educational successes of certain minorities, though this is closer to Putnam's (2000) focus on strong interpersonal bonds as a resource than to Bourdieu. Others might draw attention to the particularities of the images and stereotypes of the different ethnic categories, reflecting different histories, and therefore the different degrees and types of racism they produce. The point is there seems to be at least some aspect of people's position in the class structure and their views that is attributable to their membership of an ethnic/racial group rather than to class constraints alone.

Conceptualizing the relationship

So how have those interested in class responded and made sense of all of this? The answer is: it depends entirely on what they take class to be. If we start first of all with the Marxists, it might be supposed that for them ethnicity and race are far from autonomous sources of division and inequality but, instead, reducible to productive relations, and that is indeed the argument of some. One of the earliest and best-known analyses to this effect, echoed in more recent arguments (e.g. Balibar and Wallerstein, 1991; Callinicos, 1993), was put forward by Oliver Cromwell Cox (1948). For him, racism and ethnic conflict were born in and bound up with the long march of capitalist development – in ancient societies there had been religious divisions or divisions between citizens and slaves, but not ethnic divisions and racism as there is today. In capitalist societies there is a need to exploit ever greater labour power to accumulate capital, and so it was bound up from the start with colonialism and slave trading to put more bodies to work, but the added effect was that capitalists could whip up antagonism between black and white workers by portraying the former negatively in its ideology, splitting the proletariat against itself and quelling any chance of resistance. Some later Marxists, such as Michael Reich (1981), added that this 'divide and conquer' strategy was also accomplished through the conscious use by capitalists of impoverished black workers as strike breakers and cheap labour to undercut and antagonize white workers.

Others within the Marxist camp, however, have taken a different view. Those associated with the CCCS in the 1970s and 1980s (e.g. Hall, 1980; CCCS, 1982), for example, alongside others such as Robert Miles (e.g. Miles and Brown, 2003), sought to build a neo-Marxist view of racism that did away with crude economic reductionism. Once again structural Marxism (as well as Gramsci) was to be the saviour here, since it allows a replacement of the crude Marxist base–superstructure model of society with an image of multiple relatively autonomous domains, including ideology and politics. Racism in the UK, therefore, is bound up not just with economic oppression, though that plays its part, but with the particular form of nationalist ideology developed in Britain as a result of its declining international power and the authoritarian populist politics that sprang up in the 1980s to shore up hegemony at home. Not only that, but we need to acknowledge that the constitution of the categories of 'race' is not simply a question of one-way imposition by the oppressor, not simply 'false consciousness', but the product of struggle between racist oppression on the one hand and the resisting oppressed groups who re-appropriate labels to assert their identity ('black is beautiful') on the other.

Just as with feminism, however, the embrace of structural Marxism was but a bridge to the cultural turn and a cold-shouldering of class, this time represented most obviously by David Theo Goldberg's (1987) Foucauldian rejection of Marxism but most emblematically by a premier contributor to the CCCS line, Paul Gilroy (1987/2002). Dissatisfied with the reduction of race to ideology or politics on the grounds that it played down its specificity, Gilroy made the case that race was instead a question of culture: a distinct axis of oppression, separable from exploitation, but also an independent source of opposition to capitalism and collective political action. Just as well too, he added, joining the chorus of post-Marxists, since class struggles and politics have declined in recent years thanks to post-industrialism and so on. In fact, the very (Marxist) concept of class may need to be dispensed with, since in his eyes it would take more effort than it is worth to revise it enough to accommodate race as an autonomous principle of domination and struggle.

No such worries appear to plague Erik Olin Wright (1997), who also recognizes ethnic or racial divisions as separate, autonomous forms of oppression operating with a different logic from class, i.e. class works through exploitation, but racial conflict does not. He demonstrates this with the old colonial American saying 'the only good native American is a dead native American', which demonstrates racial tension and animosity that can culminate in genocide; but you would never get a capitalist saying 'the only good worker is a dead worker', since capitalists need workers to exist. True enough, Wright still expects and tries to show through his research that there is a strong link between class exploitation and racial oppression. For example, he finds that black workers in the US are more likely to be critical of capitalism than are white ones, partly because black workers tend to occupy more exploited positions but also partly because racial oppression in the US was so tightly bound up with class exploitation historically, specifically in the form of slavery. Yet Gilroy is right: acknowledging the autonomous existence of ethnicity as a principle of inequality, oppression and division, even if interacting with class, goes against the principles of Marxist thought – labour is, by implication, no longer the distinguishing or fundamental feature of humanity – and represents a considerable concession to Weberians, for whom ethnicity has, of course, always been separable.

At first sight the Weberian view might be that ethnicity operates as a separate division of *status* – certain ethnic groups, recognized by their particular lifestyle or way of living, are devalued in society because of a negative construction of the group arising out of the historical relation between the dominant and dominated ethnic groups in society, and this can affect their life chances through discrimination, which is separable from the constraints of income flowing from their class situations. Status and class obviously interact, as the devalued ethnic group is disproportionately pushed down into lower market and class situations which then also impact on life chances. However, Weber (1978) was actually a little more specific on the features of 'ethnic' groups, noting their anchoring in ideas of common descent and their participation in processes of closure and monopolization on a par with classes. On this basis some Weberian researchers have made the case that ethnicities are not really status groups per se, but instead potential bases of group formation in struggles for better life chances through appropriation of class or status advantages (Rex, 1986).

Either way, with labour no longer being the be-all and end-all of humanity, it becomes a bit easier to examine the interplay of class and ethno-racial domination without reductionism or contradiction. Rex and Tomlinson (1979), for example, argued that immigrants who had come to Birmingham from former British colonies in search of work, instigating extra competition and fear over jobs, were, because of imperialist ideas of racial superiority, stigmatized and shunned by the white working class in their own struggles for improved work conditions, housing and schooling. The immigrants were therefore not only pushed down into lower market situations, excluded from access to social housing and segregated and discriminated against in the education system, forming a distinct 'underclass', but had no choice but to form their own ethnic-based community groups and identities to fight their corner. Similarly, William Julius Wilson (1980) offered a broadly Weberian analysis of the relationship between race and class in the US. He controversially argued that, historically, racial oppression pushed black people into disproportionately disadvantaged positions in the class structure but that then, following the civil rights movement in the 1960s, the overt inequalities of race have declined but the constraints of the class positions they had been forced into remain – so their problem now is the class position they were forced into, not the racial oppression which put them there in the first place.

Since the 1980s, however, there have actually been very few serious investigations of how class and ethnicity interact from a Weberian point of view, perhaps because the Nuffield School cornered the market in Weberian work on class but had little time for studying ethnicity. This means the two dominant stances on the class–ethnicity nexus remain Marxism of varying shades of reductionism on the one hand, from Cox to Virdee (2014), and, on the other, post-Marxism, which essentially erases one element from the nexus altogether. There is, however, an alternative – a possible way out of the impasse – that has been steadily growing in influence in recent years, though it is nowhere near as developed as its feminist counterpart: the ideas of Bourdieu.

Bourdieu and ethnicity

Bourdieu himself said very little directly on race/ethnicity compared to class, but he did not ignore it altogether. He gave pointers or reflections here and there, and it has been left to others inspired by him to take them up, apply them in research and develop them as they see fit. One line of research, for example, has been to examine race/ethnicity as a principle of group-making: just as 'working class' is a contentious category of perception used to make sense of the divisions of social space and mobilize individuals around certain interests, so the category 'Muslim' or 'Romanian' is a discursive representation of difference with symbols, ideas, myths and supposed boundaries debated, struggled over and claimed allegiance to in opposition to others (Brubaker, 2004).

In terms of how this relates to class, the best-known argument comes from Bourdieu's collaborator in later life, Loïc Wacquant (2009). He has traced the history of 'race' as a way of describing and dividing up the world in the US, or more precisely the history of the emergence of a concept of 'blackness' – whatever variation might be contained within that term – as opposed to 'whiteness', and how it has been used to subjugate, and contain within lower zones of social space, certain sectors of the population (on the emergence of ethnic categories in colonial Europe, compare Steinmetz, 2007). First emerging to legitimize slavery, then evolving through explicit laws of racial segregation, today blackness is – thanks to media and political discourse – equated with a level of criminality and danger that only tough law-and-order measures can supposedly battle. This argument might, on first sight, seem quite Marxist. Racial categories apparently emerged to aid extraction of unfree labour, for example, and today's criminalization and imprisonment of alarming swathes of the urban black population serve the double function of (1) controlling and disciplining the most dispossessed and (2) channelling the anxieties of everyone else in the face of the labour market insecurity promoted by neoliberal politics as a strategy of capital accumulation. It has to be remembered, however, that at the root of this are all kinds of struggles for recognition, and Wacquant has stressed that the state, as a field in Bourdieu's sense, is riven by internal oppositions and conflicts; it is just that the pole dominated by the logic of economic capital as the marker of symbolic worth in society is currently dominant and so the views according with its interests prevail.

Wacquant's analysis might be a little too 'black and white', however, since it fails to make sense of why people categorized into different ethno-racial 'groups' (blacks, Hispanics, Chinese etc.) are *differentially* distributed in the social space – why some do better than others, in other words. This is partly to do with the particularities of the US's very rigid binary approach to race, inscribed in law, and in the European context the picture can be filled out a bit with the work of Bourdieu's long-time friend and collaborator Abdelmalek

Sayad (2004). He analysed what he called the 'suffering of the immigrant' lacking symbolic capital and made the sound point that to understand the position, trajectory and habitus of an immigrant in their receiving country's social space, you have to know what their position, trajectory and habitus were in their home country's social space *and* the relation between the two social spaces in the world system, or, to coin a phrase, the global social space (levels of economic development, trade and aid dependencies, historical/colonial ties and so on). When there are general patterns – migrants from different countries tending to hail from different locations in their home class structures – this might go some way towards explaining, for example, the different performance of Caribbean and Asian immigrants in the UK.

There is still a possibility that this perspective, if not Marxist, might be read as class reductionist. Wacquant is, after all, of the view that, structurally speaking, there is only the social space of capital possession – 'race' and 'class' are simply different, sometimes overlapping, ways of cutting it up in perception in line with certain interests, and for the most part definitions of 'race' seem to be imposed from above. A slightly different approach, which may well avoid that problem and which does link up to some brief remarks by Bourdieu (1991: 289n3) himself, has been pursued by researchers in Australia. Both Hage (2000) and Tabar et al. (2010) have, in slightly different ways, put forward the idea that ethnicity (or nationality in Hage's case) operates as a distinct field of struggle in itself, with – in Australia – whites of British descent occupying the dominant pole and all others clambering with greater and lesser effectiveness either to show they belong (accumulating what Hage calls 'national capital') or to assert their own worth (using what Tabar et al. call 'ethnic capital'). As with any field there are associated habitus, more or less possible moves, specific strategies, group-making, symbolic violence and all the rest.

When it comes to the relationship with class, Tabar et al. stay quiet, but Hage locates the importance of class primarily within the dominant white section of the field, which he says forms a sort of nationalist field of power. At first, in the days of colonialism, he says, there was a struggle to define whiteness, and therefore what should be valued more broadly, which pitted upper-crust British traits against a more down-to-earth working/middle-class 'Australianness', but this Australianness, after a brief spell of dominance following the downfall of Empire, has now been challenged by the rising cosmopolitan multiculturalism of those rich in cultural capital. The latter is still a mode of ethnic symbolic violence – primarily in the form of paternalism and patronization of non-whites – but it has pushed certain exclusionary versions of whiteness into a weaker, defensive position, giving rise to far-right politics as a reactionary strategy. What the intersections and struggles might look like in other countries, however, remains to be seen.

Conclusion

To sum up, then, the twists and turns in our understanding of the relationship between gender and class and between ethno-racial domination and class run remarkably parallel. In both cases the initial relationship was – and in some people's minds will always be – one primarily of antagonism, with the growing awareness of gender and ethno-racial inequalities weakening the importance and even foundations of the concept of class. Over time, however, various efforts to accommodate gender and ethnicity as relatively autonomous sources of division, interacting with class in diverse ways, have surfaced, only to succumb to the cultural turn. In Marxism, the journey from structural Marxism to post-Marxism saw class drop out of the picture, or become palatable only in a more Weberian style, yet the dominant Weberian view of class has had little appeal to those interested in cultural and symbolic struggles, discourse and identities. In both cases Bourdieu's ideas offer a way forward, but while this is perhaps more worked out in feminism than in studies of ethnicity and class, there is still much work, both conceptual and empirical, to be done.

Part II
Class Struggles

6
Social (Im)mobility

Concepts of class may well be rooted in different philosophical conceptions of what makes human beings what they are, and they may well generate high-level debate about their logical merits and deficiencies, but ultimately, like all good concepts, they are designed to do concrete explanatory work – to make sense of how and why the world is as it is. Hence we now descend from the heady heights of theoretical deliberation to consider some of the effects class is held to have and some of the struggles it produces, even if theory does not and cannot go away completely. We start with a topic that has long been seen as central to the sociological study of class, and which was in fact bound up with the very development and *raison d'être* of professional sociology as it took shape in the early to mid-twentieth century: social mobility, or the movement between classes within one's own lifetime or from parent to child. We will look at what exactly social mobility is (because different people have different views of what really 'counts' as social mobility), how it is studied, the major trends and debates of the last fifty years or so, the actual experience of movement in the class structure and, leading into the next chapter, some proposed explanations for why there is as little social mobility as there is.

First, however, let me start with a note on why sociologists study social mobility in the first place, because it can sometimes seem a bit of a dry and technical subject – it is, for the most part, about comparing numbers, tables, rates and odds, sometimes using advanced statistical techniques. Its importance cannot be exaggerated, in fact, since it essentially relates to why and how we are each where we are today – the objective chances of succeeding through the education system and gaining a graduate job at the end of it, or of setting up a business or landing a lucrative job after school – on the basis of what our parents do or did, the resources they have, the things or the people they know and the advantages and disadvantages that come from that without our even necessarily knowing it. The level of mobility in society thus strikes at the very heart of debates over what makes a good and fair social and political order. In liberal capitalist societies, for instance, the idea is supposed to be that there are no constraints on what people can do beyond their so-called 'natural' abilities. People are free to choose whether they work hard in school, put the hours in at work and climb the ladder – theoretically, anyone born anywhere can become anything. Not only that, but, say politicians, society *must* have high rates of social mobility to function efficiently, because only when all barriers have been removed can the most talented and hard-working individuals, no matter what their background, rise to the positions they are best suited to fill. This is the principle of 'meritocracy', which all major political parties in the capitalist West value dearly – the principle that only individual merit, not background, plays a part in determining social destinations. Social mobility research therefore acts as a check on how far that ideal is met in reality.

These are not the only reasons why sociologists study social mobility, of course, and they are certainly not why Marxists take an interest in it. For a long time in fact Marxists dismissed the study of social mobility completely as a 'bourgeois interest', since no matter how much movement of people there is between capital and labour the structure of class relations, and exploitation, remains the same (Poulantzas, 1975). More recently, however, Erik Olin Wright (1997) has examined it with an eye on the likelihood of class-for-itself emergence – if there is barely any movement between classes (or class locations), then perhaps people are more likely to become conscious of their common situation, band together and take action. In this he resembled the Weberians, who initially expressed interest in the formation of social classes – whether the working class or the service class – through restricted mobility chances, though that is no longer quite as central to their concerns as it once was.

As for Bourdieu, remember his notion of 'trajectory', or the fact that changes in possession of capital over time – both individual and among whole sections of the social space, and both over the generations and within one's own lifetime – are fundamental to understanding people's practices and views. We can only really get a grip on someone's current situation and habitus if we know where they, and their forebears, have come from. Hence what would be called social mobility effectively forms the third axis of social space for Bourdieu.

What is social mobility?

So if that is why sociologists study social mobility, then *how* do they study it? Unfortunately there is no real consensus here – just as there are disagreements over what class is, there are disagreements over what actually counts as social mobility and how it should be measured. However, one distinction which everyone can agree upon is that between *intra*generational and *inter*generational mobility. Intragenerational mobility means social mobility from one class to another within one's own lifetime – moving from being a bank clerk in young adulthood to a bank manager in later life, for example. Intergenerational mobility means movement between generations, so what class a person ends up in at some particular point in their life compared to the class their parents were in when they were children. The second of these is what social mobility researchers are really interested in because it best captures class inequalities rather than just career progression, but that is not to say the first is neglected altogether.

There the agreement ends, however, and on the whole we can distinguish different definitions of social mobility according to their position in relation to two debates. The first of these is whether social mobility should be seen as occurring along a continuous *scale* or between class *categories*. In the early days of research on social mobility in the US, the preferred method was to see society as made up of one long scale of prestige from top to bottom with no clear breaks separating out groups or classes. Occupations were ranked from 1 to 100 in terms of how prestigious the researchers thought they were (or sometimes on the basis of surveys of folk perception) and placed accordingly, with doctors and lawyers at the top and cleaners and factory workers at the bottom (e.g. Treiman, 1977). Individuals simply moved up or down this scale from one generation to the next like mercury in a thermometer.

Then along came Goldthorpe (1980), who pointed out that this is not really a good way of measuring patterns of social mobility at all because if there are no clear breaks between classes then we cannot capture the real qualitative shift from one type of work, one set of life conditions, experiences and constraints which can unite many occupations, to another, and that is what really matters. So Goldthorpe set out his class map with its clear boundaries, and the rest is history – it became the dominant approach in social mobility research. However, Bourdieu's perspective has recently offered an alternative, since for him social space is made up of continuous axes, capturing minute changes over time in individual resources and heterogeneity and movements within classes and occupational categories; but because it is not based on evenly spaced occupational rankings or gradations, as it was for the early US sociologists, it can also capture qualitative movements between clusters of people with similar capital, effectively integrating the best of both worlds.

The second area of disagreement has been over how many *dimensions* there are to social mobility. For those who see society as a single scale of prestige, but also for Goldthorpe, there is only really one vertical axis along which people can travel up or down. True enough, Goldthorpe does claim that there can be some degree of 'horizontal mobility' in his scheme where there is movement from one class to another with similar *rates* of life chances but a different *source* (e.g. from technical work to self-employment), but this is fairly limited in scope and usually of only marginal interest to the Nuffield School.

For the more sophisticated of the early American sociologists, on the other hand, there was more than one scale – not just prestige, but income and education level as well – and occupations and individual movements can be plotted separately on each. Each individual effectively has, therefore, multiple positions. This led to the influential idea at the time, introduced by Lenski (1954), of 'status inconsistency', sometimes also called status discrepancy, incongruence or even 'decrystallization', which tried to convey that an individual can occupy very different positions in the different hierarchies and feel the effects of that. The classic example is the teacher who has high education and prestige but a relatively low income, which might breed frustration, resentment and a desire for social change. Hence they tend to hold conspicuously liberal political views – which is as radical as politics generally gets in the US.

This approach fell out of favour partly because Goldthorpe claimed his class categories integrated all necessary elements of the different scales anyway. Yet he has actually reduced them to one dimension, albeit cut up into boxes, so there is very little scope for exploring the real differences observed between those with high education but low income and those with the reverse fortune. Once again, therefore, Bourdieu perhaps offers a more nuanced approach by including the composition of capital as a separate, horizontal axis of social space. Obviously this incorporates the kinds of things Lenski and others were getting at with status inconsistency, though Bourdieu would not put it in those terms, but importantly it also infuses with a new significance what Bourdieu calls 'transverse mobility', or mobility sideways across social space and access to a different *type* of resource and power as people invest and convert their capital into different forms – for example, wealthy businesspeople investing economic capital in private education for their children so they might develop cultural capital. In fact we can go further and recognize all sorts of movements within the social space – slopes in different directions and at different gradients as well as speeds – even if any starting point in social space has a field of more or less probable future movements built into it. This is important not least for understanding how differences of trajectory can make a difference to habitus, lifestyles and the struggles within the field of power.

Still, at the end of the day the Nuffield approach dominates social mobility research. Whichever model you prefer for theoretical reasons, however, there is an important secondary technical distinction we need to get to grips with: the difference between inflow and outflow tables. In a nutshell, *inflow* tables show the proportion of each class made up by people of different class origins, so, for example (and using Goldthorpe's terminology for convenience), how many people in the service class now are from working-class origins. *Outflow* tables, on the other hand, show where people born into each class end up, so their destinations – how many people from the working class go on to be in the service class.

If we look at tables 6.1 and 6.2, which are made up and very crude but should hopefully convey the point, you can see the inflow table tells us that 70 per cent of people *in* the service class now are *from* the service class, i.e. their father was in the service class when they were teenagers, 20 per cent are from the intermediate class and so on, whereas only 10

Table 6.1   An example of an inflow table, column percentage

Class of origin	Destination class		
	Service class	Intermediate class	Working class
Service class	70	20	10
Intermediate class	20	50	30
Working class	10	30	60
Total	100	100	100

Table 6.2   An example of an outflow table, row percentage

Class of origin	Destination class			
	Service class	Intermediate class	Working class	Total
Service class	80	15	5	100
Intermediate class	30	50	20	100
Working class	20	40	40	100

per cent of the working class is made up of people from service-class origins. The outflow table meanwhile shows us that 80 per cent of people *from* service-class origins go on to be in the service class themselves, 15 per cent fall into the intermediate class and so on, whereas only 20 per cent of the working class make it into the service class. Father's class has traditionally been taken as the yardstick, which unfortunately tends to obscure the impact of the mother's position, especially her education (or cultural capital), on social mobility. In any case, the distinction between inflow and outflow is important for testing different claims, such as the idea that the service class recruits only its own kind, and for a grasp of structural change as it takes into account the shrinking and growing sizes of classes with changes in the occupational structure – for example, more people will flow out of a class than in if that class is shrinking as occupations disappear.

Let me just mention a few more technical terms related to inflow and outflow tables which might help readers decode some of the social mobility literature. First there is the 'total mobility rate', which refers to the percentage of all people, or 'cases', who do not sit in the main diagonal of the table. Table 6.3, for example, shows numbers of people flowing between the different classes, and when we add up all those in the shaded cells and take them as a percentage of the total (600), we get a total mobility rate of 40 per cent. That is actually rather low – most total mobility rates tend to be around 60 to 70 per cent (Breen, 2004) – so this is a particularly low-mobility fictional society. We can then distinguish

Table 6.3 Working out total mobility rates

Class of origin	Destination class		
	Service class	Intermediate class	Working class
Service class	120	40	10
Intermediate class	60	120	70
Working class	20	40	120
Total	200	200	200

those cells that represent only upwards mobility or only downwards mobility and work out their rates, and then we can compare them with the rates of this society from the past or with the rates detected in other societies across the world. The second term, which starts to nudge us into more complex territory and beyond which we shall not go, is the 'index of dissimilarity' (DI or Δ), which refers to the percentage of all cases that would need to change cells, or classes, to make the table equal. Again, this index can be compared over time or between nations to track changes and variations in openness.

Trends in social mobility

Having covered the why and the what, now we can move on to look at the actual trends in mobility which have character-ized the twentieth and early twenty-first centuries. Let us start with the period from after the Second World War, when in America, where the earliest mobility research was done, there was a strong belief that the maturing capitalist order (or the 'industrial order' as they preferred to call it to distance them-selves from Marxism), with the US at its head, was character-ized by a new period of freedom and equality measurable through mobility rates. In feudalism, which had defined Euro-pean societies for centuries, one's position was *ascribed*. It was given at birth and unalterable by the individual – no one could just become a lord through effort (this is an oversim-plification, but in general it held good). In capitalism, however, where ownership is no longer tied to hereditary rights but is open to anyone, where labour is technically free and anyone can supposedly become bourgeois through enterprise or edu-cation, such constraints have, it was argued, melted away and left our position in life something to be *achieved* through hard work and talent. This, the claims went, was coupled with a technological advancement eliminating many of the lowest-skilled and lowest-paid manual jobs. The occupational struc-ture was therefore changing, with an upskilling of the workforce and a growing 'middle belt' in the class structure into which more people could move. Together these two changes were producing a rise in mobility levels, a widespread equality of opportunity and, therefore, a truly egalitarian society. Such were the assertions of people such as Talcott Parsons (1954), Daniel Bell (1973) and Clark Kerr and his colleagues (1960), and some, such as Peter Blau and Otis Dudley Duncan (1967), claimed to prove them more or less right through statistical research.

Not everyone was so cheery about the situation: some people, such as Lipset and Bendix (1959), were concerned that too much social mobility could be a bad thing, since it might well increase a sense of social dislocation and status inconsistency and therefore unsettle the social order. But it mattered little in the end – soon enough it became apparent that the declarations of an end to inequality of opportunity were somewhat exaggerated. David Glass (1954), one of the first British sociologists, provided an early counter, showing that, while there was indeed increased intergenerational mobility, most of it was very short range – just a little step up or down the ladder – and most of it occurred within the middle sections of the class structure. Very few people at the top fell from their position of privilege, and very few at the bottom managed to escape their location. Not what we would expect in a truly open, meritocratic and fair society.

However, not until the 1970s was the optimistic theory of industrial society, also known as 'liberal class theory' because of the liberalism of its proponents, actually put to the test rigorously. Britain was the place, and John Goldthorpe and his colleagues (1980, 1987) were the people to do it. By this time there certainly had been considerable occupational change, with a massive increase in white-collar work relative to blue-collar work, and Goldthorpe found that, as a result of this increased 'room at the top', upwards mobility had indeed increased and that this was long range as well as short range, with people going right from the bottom to the top and vice versa. Did this mean, then, that society *was* open, as Blau and Duncan and the others had claimed – that it was now a fair and meritocratic society to be celebrated? Not really, because Goldthorpe then made one of the most fundamental distinctions in social mobility research: that between *absolute* rates of mobility and *relative* rates of mobility.

Absolute rates of mobility refer to the total rates of upwards and downwards mobility as discussed earlier – in other words, comparing origins and destinations using inflow and outflow tables. This, said Goldthorpe, is what has increased. In pure numbers, more working-class children leave the working class than before: nearly 20 per cent make it into the top two classes (I and II) alone. But, crucially, this is the product *not* of a falling of class barriers, but of the changes in the occupational structure of society – people *had* to move away from blue-collar manual work because it was drying up; there was quite simply less to go around.

To demonstrate this he developed the notion of relative mobility rates. These measure the chances of people from certain class backgrounds attaining a particular position in the class structure relative to those from other class backgrounds – so, for example, what are the chances of a working-class youngster ending up in the service class compared to a child from the service class? When these are brought into the frame a whole different picture emerges. True enough, more people move out of the working class than before, but actually their relative chances of moving into professional occupations, compared with those from other positions in the class structure, are not much better than before. To be precise, children born into the service class were over three times more likely than those born in the working class to gain jobs eventually in the service class. True enough, too, there is more 'room at the top', but the people born at the top and near the top are filling these positions at a vastly higher rate than are the working class. We can think about this in terms of a pie: whilst the pie itself (the service class) has grown, the working class's relative *share* of the pie has not increased at all.

Sometimes this distinction is expressed in a slightly different way, especially in the US. There they contrast *structural* mobility and *exchange* mobility, with structural mobility referring to mobility that comes from changes in the occupational structure, e.g. the drying up of certain jobs and the increased room at the top forcing people to move, whereas exchange mobility refers to the actual chances of mobility stemming from one's class background, since one would actually have to exchange positions with someone else in the class structure for it to be possible.

The constant flux

Goldthorpe's next step, with Robert Erikson, was to move beyond the British context and see if this general finding stood on the global level, therefore really putting the final nail in the coffin of liberal class theory (Erikson and Goldthorpe, 1992). To do this the duo proposed to test what had become known as the 'FJH hypothesis', after the people who first forwarded it, Featherman, Jones and Hauser (1975). This hypothesis held that in all market societies characterized by a nuclear family system – an important qualification – the 'mobility regime' will be essentially the same, by which they meant the unequal patterns of *relative* mobility rates of the kind found by Goldthorpe in the UK are more or less the same *whatever the absolute rates* and are therefore a product of socio-economic structure – in other words capitalism – rather than the particular culture or occupational structure and change of any nation (whether services, manufacturing or info-tech sectors). So even the US, with all its famous rhetoric on being the land of freedom, enterprise and a lack of class barriers, would have roughly the same rates of relative mobility as the old European countries and even culturally very different societies such as Japan.

To cut a long story short, Erikson and Goldthorpe confirmed this hypothesis, the only qualification being that relative rates of mobility can be modified through express political intervention, and they coined the term 'constant flux' to capture the fact that any variation between nations or over time is of a fairly trendless nature – there is fluctuation, but it is constant and directionless. Ever since then Erikson and Goldthorpe's work has more or less set the standard for mobility studies, with some later researchers simply confirming its findings (e.g. Marshall et al., 1997) while others take issue with the message of global and historical uniformity it conveys. There are, they say, differences between nations – some, particularly former state socialist or social democratic nations but also Israel and the US, do have greater rates of mobility than others – and they have changed over time, so it is worth trying to find out why that might be (Breen, 2004). Some, most famously Wilkinson and Pickett (2009), claim rates of mobility are higher in more equal societies such as Norway and Canada – greater equality of opportunity comes with greater equality of condition, therefore – but to do so they draw on a strand of research which has become highly controversial in recent times: that of the London-based Centre for Economic Performance led by the economist Jo Blanden.

Blanden and her colleagues (2005) made the rather head-line-grabbing and politician-agitating claim that social mobility in Britain was not only worse than in many other countries but had suffered a notable decline in the second half of the twentieth century, thanks mainly to rising educational inequalities. Goldthorpe was not impressed. He soon took it upon himself to try to demonstrate why they were wrong and he was right. Their fixation on *income* mobility rather than class mobility is misleading, he said, they use completely inadequate short-term data sources and dodgy variables and they fudge the crucial difference between absolute and relative rates of mobility. If we use class categories, and if we look at relative rates within the same data, he tried to show, then it becomes apparent that the general message today is much the same as it has been for decades: there has indeed been some recent levelling-off in absolute rates of mobility in the UK, especially among men, as the occupational structure has changed (particularly the decline of skilled manual work with deindustrialization and the lack of growth in white-collar work to pick up the slack, especially as women are filling those positions at a higher rate), but the relative rates remain the same as ever (Goldthorpe and Jackson, 2007; see also Erikson and Goldthorpe, 2010; Goldthorpe, 2013). Blanden and her team (2013) have responded, however, that Goldthorpe's categories cover up important within-class differentials of income and therefore hide significant areas of decline – a point which those who lament the lack of differentiation within Goldthorpe's class scheme might sympathize with.

The experience of social mobility

So far we have been concerned with large-scale trends in social mobility as measured by statistics, reflecting the dominant themes within the field. Yet each number in the cells of a mobility table reflects so many human lives – so many biographies, experiences, hopes and desires; so many breaks from the past and entrances to new social worlds – and there has long been a strand of work interested in making sense of the effects of social mobility for individual identity and wellbeing. We already know from earlier that an initial concern among some liberal class theorists was that social mobility might be somewhat disorienting for people, as they find themselves unable to 'fit in' to their new class, i.e. the colleagues they work with, the decisions they have to make, the responsibilities they have and so on. They do not quite feel they belong, perhaps, or feel they have to work twice as hard to prove themselves since they were not born into privilege, producing all sorts of anxieties and pressures. Or as others explored, maybe social mobility comes at enormous *sacrifice* – working so hard to earn money or prestige and be 'successful' that family life and other little pleasures of this limited existence are foregone – and with tremendous amounts of *guilt* – including from a sense of having betrayed your roots, or your family, having left them behind and, at least implicitly, rejected their way of life as inferior (Sennett and Cobb, 1977).

Naturally it was Goldthorpe (1980) who set out to test some of these ideas. Using interviews and written biographical sketches from participants in his original British survey, he tried to explore just how people evaluated their movement, or lack thereof, in the class structure and what kind of impact it had on their lives. What he found was an overwhelmingly positive outlook amongst both mobile and immobile alike. Among the upwardly mobile there was a strong sense of having seized upon new opportunities and advanced – they had indeed entered novel social and cultural worlds, but in so doing had brought about a more secure and rewarding life for themselves and their family. The transition was smoothed, furthermore, by the fact that so many people had been mobile into the service class: it was not at all unusual to be from a working-class or other background, so people hardly felt like freakish outsiders. Even the immobile were generally content with their lot, focusing on how their position had still improved relative to their parents' in terms of better working conditions and higher pay. So all in all, concluded Goldthorpe, social mobility had proven to be a thoroughly rewarding experience, bolstering the generally held view that it forms an unalloyed good and, for a long time, ending the debate.

More recently, however, there has been something of a return to the more ambivalent or critical view of the effect of upward mobility, emphasizing betrayal, guilt or feelings of being a 'fraud' (see, for example, contributions to Mahony and Zmroczek, 1997), or at least a rather more modest and non-linear account of progress (Miles et al., 2011), but now underpinned by Bourdieusian as well as psychoanalytical (or 'psychosocial') themes. Bourdieu was himself socially mobile, and this left him with an acute sense of what social space travel feels like and how it can be something of a double-edged sword. It is, therefore, no surprise that he developed a whole set of phrases and concepts to try to encapsulate the experience, most of which revolve around the fact that social mobility is not just about changing types of jobs and having access to new opportunities, as it is for Goldthorpe, but about moving between totally different ways of life associated with different sections of social space (see Friedman, 2014). One of the best-known and most referred to of these phrases is 'fish out of water', capturing instances where a habitus forged in one set of conditions of existence (e.g. small-town working class) is thrust into an alien set of conditions or situations (e.g. university, professional work), with different associated lifestyle practices and values, does not know how to respond and produces intense self-consciousness – though to be honest Bourdieu himself generally only used the phrase 'fish *in* water' to describe how habitus adapts to its position, and tended instead to use the term 'hysteresis' to describe instances where habitus has not quite adjusted to new conditions.

Some of Bourdieu's more specific terms to capture the downsides of social mobility tend to emphasize the sense of being torn between two worlds. Thus he talks of the 'double isolation' of the socially mobile or parvenu – the feeling of no longer fitting in with family and friends from home, yet not feeling as though they really belong to the new world they have entered either – and the 'double bind' of the successful working-class child – the sense that in being 'successful', and fulfilling parental hopes, one has to break with and reject the parental way of being, looking down on them without wanting to, which can be extremely painful (Bourdieu, 1996, 1999b; see also Walkerdine et al., 2001). To describe his own experience, furthermore, he coined the term 'cleft habitus' (or 'habitus clivé'), which was meant to portray the fact that social mobility can produce a habitus with contradictory and clashing dispositions, some formed in the class conditions of youth, some formed in adapting to later novel experiences, and none of them sitting well together – being at once thankful to yet scornful of the education system, for example (Bourdieu, 2004b).

Others have started to confirm or work through some of these ideas. For example, van Eijk (1999) has tried to show that the socially mobile are more likely to be 'omnivorous' in their consumption patterns, mixing the musical or other tastes of their youth, which were around them constantly as they grew up and generate a sense of nostalgia and connection to the past, with new tastes picked up through subsequent experience. Having acquired cultural capital they may come to appreciate classical music, for instance, but they still like to listen to the old pop songs they danced to as children to remind them of good times. Friedman (2012), on the other hand, describes the socially mobile as 'culturally homeless' – i.e. never feeling as though their tastes are truly valid, since they feel guiltily snooty when talking music, films, comedy and so on with family and old friends but also embarrassingly common or stupid when discussing them with friends or colleagues from the newly entered zone of social space. In later work, however, Friedman (2015) has nuanced the picture by exploring how the experience of social mobility differs with speed, length and direction of trajectory – or 'slope and thrust', as Bourdieu (1984) himself put it. Where upwards mobility is gradual, relatively short range and/or tilted towards the economically rich side of social space, as in slow progression from shop floor to management in business, the experience is smoother and less problematic. Where it is rapid, long range and/or into the cultural fraction of the dominant class, on the other hand, the experience can be more disorienting and difficult.

Why does social immobility persist?

So now we come to the final question: if statistical research shows that inequalities in social mobility are deeply embedded, and that those lower down the class hierarchy suffer the same low odds of upwards mobility throughout recent history and across nations, or perhaps worse odds, *why* is this so? It is all very well pointing to the figures and experiences, but how do we explain them? One key factor in the equation has long been recognized: education. Hence the next chapter will grapple with some of the major themes and trends in class inequalities in educational performance. As a prelude to that, however, it is worth mentioning one important controversy which has occupied the minds of social mobility researchers in particular: the meritocracy debate.

There is, after all, one very straightforward theory for understanding why few working-class people leave their class of origin and why others from higher classes stay within theirs, one which is actually very popular amongst the general public, the media and politicians in one form or another, to greater or lesser degrees, and which is actually the implicit bedrock of any argument for meritocracy or equality of opportunity: perhaps some people are simply lazy, or, even more deterministically, perhaps some people simply lack the ability or the talent to rise up the social hierarchy because of their genetically inherited low intelligence.

This kind of argument might be familiar to readers who have encountered Charles Murray's views on the underclass and ethnic inequality (e.g. Herrnstein and Murray, 1994), and is implicit in much of the liberal class theory outlined earlier, but in recent times this stance has been defended most doggedly by Peter Saunders (1990, 1995, 1997; Bond and Saunders, 1999). Explicitly championing a right-wing perspective, he declared that inequality was justified and he berated mainstream sociologists of class – especially Goldthorpe, but also Richard Wilkinson – for what he called their 'left-wing bias'. Healthy capitalist societies need inequality, he argued, in order to ensure the motivation and hard work necessary for them to function properly, to spur talented people on to the top positions, and to reward ability and effort. Moreover, contemporary Britain is, he said, nearly such a healthy capitalist society. The fact is, some people are genetically more intelligent or talented than others – they inherit their 'intelligence quotient' (IQ) from their parents, perform better in school and, with a little hard work, achieve the roles that demand a high IQ such as medical, legal or academic professions. More middle-class people have a high IQ because they themselves have got to those positions because of it, and then pass it on to their children, whereas the working class tend to have a low IQ and pass this on to their children. No wonder working-class children are less likely to go on to be doctors or lawyers, then – they lack the genetic endowment. This was not all just theory, though. He tried to show through statistics that social mobility was more strongly associated with educational attainment and IQ scores than with class position. Any inequality detected by Goldthorpe and others was therefore a willed, left-wing ignorance of IQ winning through and is, at the end of the day, justified.

Enter Goldthorpe, who, with his colleague Richard Breen, decided to engage with Saunders head on (Breen and Goldthorpe, 1999, 2002; Saunders, 2002). His primary tactic was to beat Saunders through technical sophistication: if you use this statistical test rather than the one Saunders has used, you find that, lo and behold, class position is a better predictor than IQ of social mobility after all, meaning there must be something to class itself which directs life paths, namely, the economic resources and constraints that attach to the different class categories as a result of their employment relationship – whether they have the ample means and stability of a service relationship or the insecurity and low reward of a labour contract. It is not having the money, or more precisely not having parents who have the money, to afford not to work and to stay on at school, to pay fees for further or higher education, or to pursue particular entrepreneurial avenues, irrespective of their IQ, that prevents people from climbing the ladder, as they have rationally decided that the risks outweigh the likely payoff. The only way we will ever achieve real meritocracy, or equality of opportunity, therefore, is to reduce the arbitrary economic constraints people face, and the only secure way to guarantee this, argues Goldthorpe, is through equality of condition, i.e.

the redistribution of economic wealth and equalization of incomes.

Goldthorpe and his followers seemed to have the last word in this debate – Saunders, volubly disgusted by the vilification he felt he faced, abandoned academia altogether and opted to become a pen-for-hire for right-wing think tanks. But we might want to ask whether the debate was justified at all, because from a Bourdieusian point of view, arguing over whether economic factors or intelligence are better predictors of social mobility misses the point: intelligence, when we break away from the genetic theory Saunders adheres to and recognize it as a social endowment passed on through socialization, as cultural capital, *is class*. The research of Leon Feinstein (2003), an educational psychologist who looked at long-term trends in child development, is worth mentioning here. He found that while there are differences in ability between children on various tests at early stages of life – which in themselves confirm neither genetic nor sociological explanations – these were far from set in stone, and therefore were unlikely to be the causal motor of future success as Saunders would have it. Instead they were utterly changeable according to class position. No matter what the performance level at 22 months old, children born to affluent professional parents were likely to perform well at later stages right into adulthood, whereas those born to poorer parents, again no matter what their early performance, did less well – in fact those who performed really poorly in the affluent class often ended up overtaking those who performed very well in the working class – suggesting that it is through ongoing socialization rather than genetic ability that people develop the ways of thinking valued and rewarded within the education system.

In short, unequal 'intelligence', or 'talents', i.e. cultural capital, are themselves the product of unequal social conditions, and so arguing for intelligence's determining power is arguing for the power of class – just a particular element of it – not against it. This means, of course, that the whole idea of meritocracy is utterly flawed, because it will only ever reward that which is already possessed by the privileged and perpetuate existing inequalities. In fact, it serves rather well to cover up this perpetuation and legitimize it in the eyes of the populace by falsely painting it as survival of the brightest. Bourdieu calls this a 'sociodicy of privilege', by analogy with a theodicy, which is an attempt to explain how evil can exist in a world overseen by a benevolent god: meritocracy is a convenient means of explaining and justifying how and why inequality and reproduction of privilege exist in a supposedly fair and benevolent social system, i.e. capitalism. To explore this further, however, we need to dig a little deeper into the workings of the education system and its thorny relationship to class.

7
Educational Reproduction

The official, political rhetoric surrounding education has long been that it can, should and does serve as a source of liberation, offering people from any walk of the life the opportunity to 'make it' and be somebody. For about as long, however, sociologists have been showing it to be one of the most fundamental mechanisms through which inequalities are perpetuated and legitimated over the generations, and since there is a good chance that you – the kind of person who would read this kind of book – are, like me, a part of the education system, some of the ways in which this manifests in everyday experience should be all too tangible. It is inherent in the marks that teachers and lecturers give to their students and the casual judgements they pass on them – someone is a 'good student' and 'bright', another 'tries hard' but 'doesn't get it' while another is 'a troublemaker' or 'a bit dim' – but also walking around university campuses where a certain accent, way of dressing, talking, acting and thinking seems preponderant (especially to those with different accents, ways of dressing and so on), to different degrees in different institutions of course.

There are two important developments contextualizing all sociological work on the connection between class and education. The first is the steady growth through the twentieth century of the education systems of all major Western societies, pulling in more and more young people and keeping hold of them for longer and longer. Up until the nineteenth century schooling was a fairly haphazard affair provided privately, or by bourgeois philanthropists and the church who took it upon themselves to provide some form of basic training and education to the poor. With the deepening of the Industrial Revolution and the birth of capitalism, after all, it became desirable for workers to have at least a modicum of knowledge in order to labour adequately, though any education beyond the most elementary level still seemed an unnecessary extravagance. The story of the last hundred years or so, however, is of schooling increasingly being made compulsory and delivered by the state and of raising the mandatory leaving age, and then universities and colleges proliferating and expanding as affluent, technologically advanced, protectionist nation states demanded an ever more skilled and educated workforce to deliver the political goal of economic growth. This latter trend has been intensified by globalization: as industrial work was shipped out of the West and national economies progressively specialized in a global division of labour, politicians in post-industrial nations such as those in Europe increasingly made the case that it was necessary to ensure reproduction of a highly educated home workforce capable of providing the niche technical, intellectual and financial services on the world market if their economies were to thrive and people be kept in jobs.

Bound up with this political aim was the emergence of the idea of 'human capital' in economics, i.e. the idea that the knowledge, skills, abilities and characteristics of human beings can be measured in terms of their ability to produce economic value and that they can and must be nurtured through economic investment, such as through building more schools and universities. Not only that, but to drive up standards some Western governments, such as the UK and US, decided to introduce market forces into the educational system by giving parents free choice over which schools they can send their offspring to rather than it being pre-set, the logic, derived from the dominant neoliberal mindset, being that all schools will improve in the competition – never mind the fact that in order to have competition and winners you have to have losers, and that the 'losers' are not just throwaway consumer products but institutions directing people's entire futures. There has also been the introduction of numerous forms of more or less independent schools, run by businesses, charities, individuals or groups of parents, the belief being that they will run schools more efficiently than the state and widen choice further.

The result of all this educational expansion and rising standards, say some, has been a breakdown of class barriers. More people than ever before are experiencing a once exclusive thing, leaving their home environment and making choices and assessing options that were previously foreclosed. As we have already seen, Beck (1992) and Archer (2007) claim that novel educational opportunities and experiences have helped usher in a new age of individualization or reflexivity, in which people's class backgrounds are overcome by the reflexive decisions they have to make about their futures in the face of new information and possibilities, while others have suggested that if there is any division to speak of it is a simple case of winners versus losers in the new scenario, the losers being a minority (Lash and Urry, 1994). These ideas are tempered, however, by the second development, which proceeded in tandem with the first: the deepening internal stratification of the educational system.

The twisted legacy of Darwinism and eugenics (the belief that genetically weak individuals should be prevented from having children) in the late nineteenth and early twentieth centuries was a widespread belief that intelligence is more or less genetic – we saw in the last chapter there are still many who make this case today. On the assumption that economic efficiency would come from having the most talented people in the most demanding jobs, and that the talent (or 'merit') may lie anywhere undetected, national state education systems were designed to channel young people in different directions from the very start on this basis, in all cases distinguishing those apparently more suited to *academic* training (the valorized pathway to success and power) and those more suited to *practical* training (the generally disparaged pathway to lower-paid and lower-esteemed work), with a more advanced *technical* training often lying in between. The ways and means of doing that are enormously varied, more or less explicit and cross-cut by a gendered division between masculine 'hard' subjects (physics, maths, information technology or woodwork, metalwork etc.) and feminized 'soft' subjects (social sciences, arts, languages or childcare, beauty therapy etc.), but they all boil down to the basic opposition between the academic and the practical, or the abstract and the concrete.

It could be that children are formally assessed and streamed by exam – as in the UK in the 1960s with the 11+ exam, or the Zhongkao exam in China – or it could be self-selection, with children choosing different pathways on the basis of what they believe themselves to be 'good at'. It could be, and often is, that young people are filtered into entirely different institutions, with some schools specifically preparing them for university through studying arts, sciences, literature, languages – the old English grammar schools, the German *Gymnasium* and the French *lycée général* are all good examples – while others focus on the teaching of practical skills and preparation for the world of relatively unskilled work for boys or home management for girls – the old English secondary moderns, German *Hauptschule* and French *lycée profesionnel* fit this bill – or at best higher technical or vocational skills, as with the old English technical schools and the German *Realschule*. Or it could be that children are streamed within an institution, especially in systems which are supposedly 'universal' such as the current UK comprehensive schools or US high schools – people are put in different 'sets' on the basis of their perceived ability or choose different options for their exams, whether GCSEs in most parts of the UK, baccalaureates in France and Spain or whatever. And this is without even mentioning the parallel existence of private schooling in most countries, which, because of the exorbitant fees they now charge to keep ahead, alongside the endowments given by wealthy benefactors, possess resources that state schools can only dream of, such as smaller class sizes, better facilities, more trips, special equipment, more highly educated teachers and greater links with universities.

Now whatever the sentiment behind these various ways of cutting up the education system to channel children down different tracks, they essentially served to translate class differences into educational differences, with children from more advantaged backgrounds heading by the academic pathway on to university, and the less advantaged being consigned to practical studies and leaving school much earlier to take up paid work. Both Bourdieu, in his early work with Jean-Claude Passeron (1977/1990), and the Nuffield School demonstrated this early on. The latter, for example, in research headed by A. H. Halsey (Halsey et al.,1980), provided some of the clearest and most rigorous statistics on the persistence of class differences through the post-war education boom in the UK (the Coleman Report did something similar in the US: Coleman et al., 1966). The findings were hardly easy reading for politicians, because the team found that at every single step of the way – getting into grammar school, choosing to stay on at school until age 18 or attending university – those who benefitted most were not the working class, as was hoped, but the middle classes. Just to give one example: whilst children from both the working class and service class increased their chance of going on to university, around a quarter of all those in the service class now went on to university – an increase of 20 per cent from before educational expansion – but only 3 per cent of the working class went, a paltry number on its own and an increase of just 2 per cent after all the supposed moves towards meritocracy.

The only stage at which some equality had been achieved was in staying on to do exams at age 16 (at the time they were not compulsory, so people had to choose to stay on). It was not a case of doing *well* at 16, or continuing in education afterwards, but of simply sitting one's exams at 16, whatever the grades. But, said Halsey and his team, this was due to the fact that levels of skill and knowledge which would previously have been gained at work were now being credentialized, so that people could no longer get the jobs they would have done in the past unless they acquired these qualifications. All this was regardless of IQ, since the Nuffield collective controlled for that. It was, Halsey et al. said, material circumstances – class and wealth – which were the best predictors of outcomes and exposed the failure to provide equality of opportunity.

The grammar school system studied by Halsey et al. has long gone (mostly), but more recent data show that inequality persists, with those with parents in the top class of the NS-SEC being almost twice as likely as those with parents in the bottom class to attain good GCSEs of the kind that will see them into further academic study and university, and the differences being staggered gradually in between (ONS, 2010). Figures from the Youth Cohort Study also confirm the disparities in the chances of being in full-time education (essentially, university) at age 19 and the reverse pattern of likelihoods of being 'NEET' at the same age – this is the UK government's acronym for 'not in education, employment or training' at all, something of a demonized category (table 7.1). Similar figures can easily be found with comparable measures for other countries in Europe, North America, Australia and New Zealand.

Moreover, as charted by Bourdieu (1996; Bourdieu and Passeron, 1979) in France and Reay et al. (2005) in the UK, the process of internal stratification and its class consequences have seeped into the higher education system too, with institutions and subject areas being seen as more or less 'prestigious' and thus more or less valuable, again closely matching the divisions between academic and vocational or applied studies (and university specialisms) and between hard and soft disciplines and, once again, corresponding very closely to class background. Even if working-class youngsters get into university, in other words, there is a distinct chance that the institution they enter and the subject they study will leave them with a degree which carries less prestige on the labour market. Meanwhile the more advantaged, as well as attending more highly esteemed institutions, are also increasingly turning to postgraduate qualifications as a way to distinguish themselves from the masses (Wakeling, 2005).

Table 7.1 Educational inequalities in the UK

NS-SEC of head of household	Per cent in full-time education at 19	Per cent 'NEET' at 19
Higher professional	61	5
Lower professional	55	9
Intermediate	41	13
Lower supervisory	31	13
Routine	30	23

Source: Youth Cohort Study 2011

How, then, have class researchers tried to explain the persistence of class inequalities in the face of educational expansion? There are three approaches, which just so happen to match the three major schools of thought in class theory: Marxism, Weberian approaches – including Goldthorpe's rational action theory – and Bourdieu and the Bourdieusians. Let us take each in turn.

Marxism: education as domination and emancipation

For Marxists the expansion of education and the continued class disparities in outcomes are easy to explain: they simply reflect a new method of keeping workers down and reproducing labour power. Capitalism, after all, needs docile and obedient yet skilled workers, and where better to nurture them than in the education system? The major theoretical statement to this effect came from Louis Althusser (1971), who wrote a famous essay on the role of the state in maintaining bourgeois domination. There are, he said, 'repressive state apparatuses', such as the police, the army and the courts, which serve to quell disorder and resistance through punitive means, but there are also 'ideological state apparatuses' which function to keep the system going through indoctrination of one sort or another, and the education system – from nursery to university – is a (if not the) prime example.

Althusser was a little sketchy on the details, but the general idea was taken up and developed most famously by two American economists, Samuel Bowles and Herbert Gintis (1976). They argued that schooling manages to prevent resistance and reproduce capitalist relations in a number of ways. Most obviously it instils the skills necessary for production to continue, but it also legitimates class inequality through the ideology of meritocracy, fragments and weakens the working class by fostering status distinctions between them (high and low 'achievers') and, crucially, produces and rewards personality traits enabling smooth work relations. This last function was said to be served through the 'close correspondence' between the social organization and relationships of the school and those of the world of paid employment. There is, in other words, a 'hidden curriculum' – a phrase coined by a like-minded thinker, Michael Apple (1978) – embedded not so much in the content of the lessons as in the very way in which schooling is delivered. The fact that there is a hierarchy of teachers and headteachers, or superiors, whose bidding children, the subordinated, must do, for example, prepares the latter to follow the orders of managers and employers dutifully at work. Children are, moreover, oriented towards 'external rewards' from the get-go, i.e. encouraged to work at school not for the love of learning or self-realization but to beat others in the competition for qualifications, preparing them to value work simply as a means to the end of earning more money rather than for the intrinsic satisfaction of labour (since that would alert them to their alienation).

There were further nuances to this argument. For instance, Bowles and Gintis claimed that the differentiation of schools and the emerging internal stratification of the higher education system, all corresponding to different sections of the class structure, served to integrate the different types of workers necessary for capitalist production (plumbers, drivers, managers, accountants etc.) in their own peculiar ways. Bowles and Gintis also recognized that the current state of affairs was not simply imposed from above but the outcome of class struggle – a compromise in the face of clashing interests over education, in other words – and that, ironically, the system generated its own critics by enabling access to forms of knowledge allowing insight into the workings of capitalism and how to challenge it. The task, in their eyes, was to try to maximize access to this knowledge and thence the chances of socialist revolution by encouraging teachers to foster class consciousness in the classroom.

Bowles and Gintis soon came under fire, not only from non-Marxists but from within Marxism itself, on the grounds that they *assumed* this passive taking on of social relations, this indoctrination through blind obedience and observation of the school's rules and authority, but never actually investigated first-hand whether this was the case at all beyond a few statistics (Sarup, 1979; Apple, 1982). If we actually go to the schools, sit with the pupils and witness their behaviour there, we might see a rather different image emerge – and this is, in fact, exactly what another Marxist, Paul Willis (1977), did. He essentially hung around with a bunch of working-class boys from the English Midlands, or the 'lads' as he called them, observing their behaviour at school and interviewing them about it. Far from complying with the rules and relationships there, he found, they developed a *counter-school culture* in which they routinely misbehaved, played truant, berated teachers and pupils who conformed and devalued academic success, 'pen-pushing' or 'mental' work, instead valuing smoking, drinking, stylish clothes, sex, fighting skill, 'having a laugh', earning their own money as a sign of independence and, ultimately, doing what they perceived to be real, masculine, manual labour. Hence they left school as soon as they could to take up work, where the counter-school culture was turned into a shop-floor culture of mild rebellion against bosses. So educational inequalities and labour power are reproduced, but only as an unintended consequence of the lads' consistently oppositional, rebellious behaviour.

Why, though, did the lads develop this oppositional culture in the first place? Willis is of the view that it stems from what he calls a 'partial penetration' of their place in capitalist society. 'Penetration' refers to awareness of their conditions of life, a bit like class consciousness for Marx, but Willis is of the view that this generally only exists at a practical, tacit, unspoken level of consciousness. So the lads know the jobs available to them are all generally the same and that sacrificing good times for a qualification that will ultimately get them a similar position anyway is hardly worthwhile; their rejection of schoolwork is a sort of 'instinctive' realization that labour power is unique in that it is a commodity that can be withheld; their valuation of dancing, fighting and so on is an effort to find freedom in the part of themselves not absorbed in production; and their subversion of school timetables is a rejection of bourgeois efforts to standardize time as a measure of labour power. This penetration is only *partial*, however, because the lads' rejection of feminized mental labour and the workings of ideology mislead them into celebrating manual work and cementing their own exploitation.

Willis' study has been immensely influential, but the discovery of the lads' counter-school culture tends to mask the rather weak explanation given for its origins – and indeed his book is a story of two halves, with the first a clear and compelling overview of the lads' behaviour and the second a highly abstract theoretical treatise almost completely detached from the ethnographic data. The fact is, the data does not actually provide direct evidence for the specifically Marxist elements of his theory, which rests on a rather far-fetched and undemonstrated assessment of how much about the capitalist system the lads seem to be aware of (with the convenient proviso that it operates at a practical level), and he fails to explain much of the lads' precise culture (Why do they value fighting? Why dancing? Why certain clothes or music?) except through a vague reference to freedom. With a Bourdieusian hat on, and anticipating arguments to come, much of the lads' behaviour, and their own testimonies, can be read instead as an effort to impose the forms of recognition they can gain access to (e.g. physical capital) as legitimate given their exclusion from the officially sanctioned forms of recognition, with the former ultimately flowing from proximity to necessity and the practical mastery and shorter-term temporal horizons it generates rather than notions of labour power.

There are other limits to Willis' study. It is, for example, based largely on a sample of just twelve boys. Can we really generalize the mechanisms of the widespread reproduction of working-class culture and educational 'failure' from such a small and, as Willis himself admits, fairly atypical group of males? What about girls, who tend to do better at school than boys (cf. McRobbie, 1991)? What about all the different subcultures within the school and indeed within the working class? After all, the pupils that the lads berated for trying hard at school (calling them 'ear 'oles' because all they did was listen to teachers) were themselves from the working class, so why were they so different? Was it perhaps a question of different levels of valued resources *within* the class, with the lads merely occupying the least privileged section (cf. Jenkins, 1983; Mac an Ghaill, 1994)? There is also a sense in which Willis' study was very much of its time – with subsequent deindustrialization and feminization of employment in the West, those sticking to the kinds of practices valued by the lads struggle to find a place in the new world of work at all, challenging or at least requiring specification of the argument that counter-school culture is a response to and reproduces indistinct labour power (see Dolby and Dimitriadis, 2004).

Despite its flaws, however, Willis' study still remains prominent and, in fact, seems to have been the last major Marxist analysis of education in sociology. Nowadays those faithful to Marx seem to assume the system is bad without really exploring how, and instead – following Marx's declaration that theory should be used to change the world rather than just interpret it – expend their efforts trying to outline an alternative, critical pedagogy in the service of emancipation. Elements of this cause can be found in Gramsci, but it was the Brazilian educator Paolo Freire (1970) who led the charge, criticizing prevailing 'banking' views of education – which see it as a process of filling people up with existing knowledge – and encouraging dialogue and the awaking of critical consciousness. These ideas have more contemporary advocates, such as Peter McLaren in the US, but over time they tended to broaden out from the Marxist base to cover other forms of oppression and eventually, reproducing the story of Marxism in general, took a postmodern turn in the work of Henry Giroux. In any case, from a strictly sociological point of view Marxism has declined in relevance and left just two key perspectives on class and educational inequalities battling for supremacy.

Weberians: secondary effects and rational choices

The first of these is the Weberian approach. Initially the best-known view on education in the post-war West grounded in Weber's thought came from Randall Collins (1979), who argued that the expansion of the system had nothing to do with equipping workers with new skills, since these could easily be learnt on the job, but was simply a new means of maintaining closure at the top of the class structure. These days, however, the most prominent perspective indebted in some way to Weber is that of John Goldthorpe, who seeks to explain why relative inequalities in educational attainment have persisted despite the growth of the system. As already seen, Goldthorpe and some of his followers have embraced a version of rational action theory in which people are seen to be making cost–benefit analyses in response to the resources they possess (see especially Goldthorpe, 2007a; Jackson et al., 2007). In elaborating this specifically for educational inequality, he borrows a distinction drawn by French sociologist Raymond Boudon (1974), another thinker sympathetic to rational choice theory, between *primary* and *secondary* effects of class stratification. Primary effects of stratification refer to anything shaping 'ability', whether social (childrearing) or genetic (IQ). Now these things do have some kind of impact, say Boudon and Goldthorpe, but they are nowhere near as important as the impact of secondary effects. In fact, if there were no primary effects at all, miraculously enough, no differences in so-called intelligence or anything like that, secondary effects would still produce inequality of educational attainment.

So what are secondary effects? Not just the direct economic constraints of class position, though that feeds into them – Boudon and Goldthorpe see things as a bit more complex than that. Basically, they are the effects that stem from *the very existence of structural stratification* – the fact that people occupy different positions in a class hierarchy. If we take for granted that people want to avoid downwards mobility and reproduce or improve their starting position, then we see that the costs and benefits of different movements within the system become very different. For the service-class child, the cost of downwards mobility (in the form of lost income over their lifetime) is greater than the costs required for the education which would prevent it (fees, time out of the labour market and so on), i.e. they would fall further than they have to climb, so for them the rational choice is to pursue education and achieve a higher-level occupation. For the working-class child, in contrast, because the effort required to reproduce their current position is less than that of a middle-class youngster (they have no need to pay educationa fees to get manual work), but to attain social mobility would cost a lot considering the low payoff (they can reproduce or slightly improve their position in much cheaper ways), the rational choice is to finish education and get a job, or maybe a skill through an apprenticeship, which is often subsidized. Of course many working-class youngsters do progress on, and we have to factor in precise resources and also self-perceived ability, admits Goldthorpe, if we are to make sense of the individual's calculation of probabilities and risks, but the fact remains that a working-class young person has to have much higher aspirations than a child from the service class to reach the same destination since they would have to travel further. On the other hand, we can easily make sense of how educational expansion has changed absolute but not relative participation or success rates in so far as it has involved a change in the structure of opportunities and costs (e.g. through student loans) for *all* classes. The only way to battle relative differences in schooling and higher education uptake is simple: we need to flatten the class hierarchy.

So what is wrong with this model? Apart from the general issues with rational action theory, there is a sense in which Goldthorpe seems to *assume* some things which should be explained – the desire to reproduce or improve one's position (and with that the very fact that certain positions and possessions are valued and to different degrees), perceptions of what is possible, differences in 'ability' and such like. This follows the general trend within rational action theory to avoid explaining differences in 'preference structures' – an aversion which Goldthorpe insists sociology in general (by which he seems to mean Talcott Parsons) is guilty of, but others would disagree. Also, in more recent work Bukodi and Goldthorpe (2013) have examined the effects of different aspects of 'social origins' on educational attainment, and while they find the effects of class (as they measure it) persist, indicating the role of economic resources, and status distinctions (as they measure them) have declined, the role of parental education and thus 'cultural resources' (help with homework, knowledge of the system etc.) is also significant and distinct from class. This is a considerable concession to an alternative position on educational inequality of which Goldthorpe has been virulently critical, one in which education and cultural resources are seen as constitutive of class rather than competing against it as a causal factor. This other position is the second of the two key perspectives currently holding court in the sociology of education, and the one becoming the dominant player: that of Pierre Bourdieu and those influenced by him.

Bourdieu: permanence through change

Bourdieu was for a long time best known for his theory of educational inequality, written with his former collaborator, Jean-Claude Passeron (1977/1990, 1979), but that has not stopped it being massively misunderstood – thanks in no small part to Bourdieu and Passeron themselves, who decided to write much of this work in impenetrable prose, but also to the fact it emerged at the height of structural Marxism's time in the sun. Some thus decry it as just another version of Marxism, some name it 'Reproduction Theory' and caricature it, some lump it together with similar but slightly different ideas put forward by an English sociologist, Basil Bernstein (1971), and so on. Even Goldthorpe, one of Bourdieu's most severe critics, openly confesses to being unable to understand what the latter is talking about half of the time.

Yet Bourdieu's theory is, in itself, relatively straightforward. First of all, remember that dominant class fractions possess plenty of cultural capital – education, awareness of high cultural forms, but above all an ease with abstraction, i.e. an ease and familiarity with the language of theoretical ideas, logical relations and concepts transcending concrete things and events. The dominated possess less. Because of this, parents who have a lot of cultural capital socialize their children differently from those who do not, intentionally and unintentionally teaching them ways of thinking and talking – pulling out logical relations, using extended vocabularies, locating experiences in formal bodies of thought, searching for 'deeper meanings' and the rest of it – through play and conversation in everyday life. The child therefore ends up with symbolic mastery, the ability and inclination to handle abstract ideas and language, or what is usually called 'intelligence', before they even enter school. Those with less cultural capital and greater proximity to necessity, however, are unable to foster this and instead their children gain a 'practical mastery' – an awareness of how concrete things work in practice, in everyday experience, knowledge by hand, but they are less able to enunciate the theoretical logic behind it or to engage with forms of knowledge based purely on symbolic mastery.

The trouble is, say Bourdieu and Passeron, the *raison d'être* of the school system is to instil, channel and reward symbolic mastery, misperceived as innate academic ability, talent or gift, yet its mode of teaching already assumes a degree of symbolic mastery. So those who have symbolic mastery thanks to their parents are already able to receive the school's pedagogy, taking to it like ducks to water, and build on their capacities; they then come to enjoy academic work in so far as a capacity to manipulate breeds ease and familiarity. Consequently – and this is important for Bourdieu – they attune their perception of their future to what is probable given their resources and mastery, meaning they tend to take it for granted as the most natural thing in the world that they will continue on to university. This is sometimes rendered in terms of 'subjective expectations of objective probabilities'.

Those with practical mastery, on the other hand, have not had the social training producing the capacities the school sees as innate and are thus less equipped to adapt to its pedagogy. They are streamed, put in bottom sets at school and ultimately filtered down vocational routes because they are labelled as not as 'bright' as other children – they are, in other words, seen as failures in terms of the ethos of the educational system. They then either accept their failure because they buy in to the official rhetoric that 'talent' should be rewarded and see themselves as 'thick', or at least unable, or else they resist like Willis' lads, come to value the practical mastery or other resources they do possess – technological or vocational skills (carpentry, metalwork or being a mechanic), sporting prowess or family – and try to pursue these, or reject school altogether as a load of rubbish, in essence rejecting only that which has already rejected them anyway.

From a historical point of view Bourdieu argues that the expansion of schooling therefore operates as little more than a new form of maintaining domination over time. Whereas once it was through the inheritance of economic capital, or before that the symbolic capital of feudal nobility, now it is through the passing on of cultural capital, and whilst at first the wealthy could invest their economic capital in private education and create cultural capital for their offspring, now there is less need for private schooling as the next generation of the dominant can pass on the cultural capital created through that initial investment.

Now Bourdieu and Passeron's argument was not without its empirical foundations, but it did remain at a fairly abstract level. Thankfully others have since fleshed out and demonstrated much of what they had to say through detailed investigation of parenting practices and schooling, especially in the US and the UK. Annette Lareau (2003), for example, famously explored through observational research the different ways in which middle-class parents and working-class parents socialize their children, producing stark differences in performance at school. Amongst the middle classes, rich in economic, social and cultural capital, she identified an approach she labelled 'concerted cultivation', involving paying for lots of capital-building extra-curricular activities and tuition for their offspring as well as teaching them rules of logic, rhetoric and vocabulary in everyday play and conversation without even intending to. On the other hand, amongst the working class she detected an approach that seems authoritarian – not knowing how to explain things grasped in practice in abstract terms, they simply say answers to homework questions are right 'because they are', 'that's the way it is' or 'because I said so' – but also oriented to the 'natural growth' of children: without the resources for activities or the time for involved play they let the children do their own thing, give them autonomy, let them play outside with friends, and rather fatalistically believe they will achieve their potential on their own or through the school's teaching alone. Lareau did, however, note that parental cultural capital was not an automatic guarantor of success since it can remain 'unactualized' – for example, there may be books in the house, but they are never read, or one parent may be highly educated, but they are always too busy or too tired to help with homework or enunciate the logical principles of this or that (cf. Lahire, 2011).

Similar patterns have been found by Walkerdine and Lucey (1989), Vincent and Ball (2007) and Devine (2004), while Diane Reay (1998) has shown how parents, particularly mothers, in the dominant class, because they know how, can and do invest much more effort and energy in their children's schooling than do the dominated (challenging teachers, taking charge of homework and so on), as well as holding much higher expectations in tune with the capital they know their children do (or will) possess. Stephen Ball (2003), applying Bourdieu's logic to more contemporary developments, has documented the range of strategies and advantages the capital-rich mobilize in the new context of school 'choice' – not only moving house to get into the catchment areas of high-performing schools, but accessing information, tapping social networks and so on to get ahead and make sure they choose the best school. All of this the dominated cannot and do not do – they tend to send their children to the nearest local school because it is what they know and it seems the most practical option. Even where children from relatively capital-rich families do attend poorly performing urban state schools, moreover, this is often driven by the desires of parents endowed with cultural capital that their children come into contact with ethnic difference and diversity (thus, in its own way, enhancing symbolic mastery of culture and social relations), and distinct class-based friendship clusters develop in the schoolyard soon enough anyway (Reay et al., 2011).

Despite this wide support, however, Bourdieu's model of educational reproduction is regularly criticized on the grounds that it is too simplistic, ignores too many intervening factors and cannot account for the increasing participation of working-class youngsters in higher education since their lack of cultural capital should have steered them away from it (e.g. Connell, 1983; Jenkins, 2002; Goldthorpe, 2007b). Yet there is far more space for complexity than is often assumed. For example, since cultural capital is a *relative* possession, not a simple binary of 'haves' and 'have-nots', all manner of shades of difference can exist between individual situations. It is not as if those in the dominated class never build *any* symbolic mastery, furthermore, just that it is self-acquired rather than 'inherited' to a greater degree and therefore less confident and less elaborate. In fact, Bourdieu argued, those in the upper sections of the dominated class and the petite bourgeoisie are disposed to precisely this self-accumulation for purposes of advancement, and certainly a frequent finding is that those who are apparently upwardly mobile, the so-called 'bright but poor', far from giving credibility to the pervasive sociodicy of meritocracy, often possess hidden resources and particular dispositions to self-accumulate symbolic mastery and cultural capital because of their slightly higher position in the social space than others within the dominated class, opening up a slightly different range of conceivable futures (Jackson and Marsden, 1962; Bourdieu and Passeron, 1977/1990; Atkinson, 2010). Bourdieu's wider social theory also allows for the impact of many intervening, mediating and complicating factors, such as the recognition that schools sit within their own space of struggle, with dominant and dominated institutions (cf. Bourdieu, 1996); that a school itself can act as a field of struggle between educators to define the correct ethos of the institution, and between educators and students (this is sometimes called 'the school effect'); and finally that family relations constitute a field of struggle over what is right and what should be done (Atkinson, 2011b, 2012a, 2014). All of these can act to complicate or specify trajectories through the educational system and the social space more generally.

As to the expansion of higher education, changes in funding and information provision may well have brought it further into the realm of objective and thus subjective possibility for larger sections of the class structure – including top slices of the dominated class – so there is no reason why that would refute a Bourdieusian approach, but there are, as studies by Archer et al. (2003) and Reay et al. (2005) amongst others make clear, a few factors to bear in mind. First, a pervasive political discourse of raising 'aspirations' without equalizing resources can engender a mismatch of subjective expectations and objective probabilities – hence higher rates of people entering university have been accompanied by higher rates of people dropping out of university. Second, class differences have become retranslated into those differences between institutions and subject areas already discussed, with working-class young people gravitating towards local, vocation-centred, newer and often devalued universities on the basis of a sense of 'fit' with their habitus while the capital-rich feel more 'at home' in the older, more academic, prestigious universities. As having a degree becomes less of a mark of distinction, these differences begin to make more of a difference. Finally, we must not forget that large swathes of the dominated class still see university as 'not for them' and aspire to work or family commitments instead.

Conclusion

Despite considerable changes in education systems around the world, it is, as Goldthorpe likes to say, an 'established phenomenon' that class inequalities, however one might want to measure them, persist, not only in the familiar form of continued relative disparities in attainment and rates of uptake of further and higher education but also, increasingly, within the higher education sector itself. In a nutshell, the *nature* of class differences may have changed, but not their existence. When it comes to explanation, Marxists no longer seem to be in the business of trying to provide any worked-out analysis of today's educational climate: Bowles and Gintis and Willis having essentially said all that needed to be said for them almost forty years ago (with Erik Olin Wright and others recently praising a reissue of Bowles and Gintis' book as just as relevant today as ever). This leaves just two perspectives on class inequalities in education: rational action theory and Bourdieu's approach. Both include a focus on the adaptation of perceptions of what is possible and desirable to the pathways opened up by possession of specific resources – and indeed there are those out there who believe the two theories have more in common than is often supposed, or could be integrated in some way (e.g. Glaesser and Cooper, 2014). Goldthorpe's recent concession that cultural resources are as key as the economic ones provided by class as he measures it only seems to buttress that argument. Yet the differences are considerable. What Goldthorpe puts aside – 'ability' (and perception of ability) – is a crucial part of the explanatory picture for Bourdieusians, and what Goldthorpe assumes – the differential ranking of ways of thinking as more and less legitimate, and thus remunerated – is both arbitrary and part and parcel of class domination today for Bourdieu. But perhaps the key fault line is in how they envision decision-making: one views people as seeking to optimize their outcomes in some way, considering costs and benefits in however limited a fashion and perceiving their own choice as rational; the other sees them as generally doing what feels 'right', 'natural' or 'for them', whether that be deliberated or not, built up through past experience and tacit knowledge of their limits. Currently, the weight of qualitative research evidence on this tends to be with Bourdieu.

8
Health, Life and Death

There are few things we value more than our health, or the health of those we care for, but the sad truth revealed by generations of social scientists is that ill-health and early death are not simply a case of fate, lottery or genetics but deeply entwined with our position in society. To be more precise, *class* position – however it might be measured – is widely recognized as perhaps the single most important driver of health outcomes in most nations across the globe (Cockerham, 2013). Exactly how it produces those outcomes is a cause of much debate, but that bare fact by itself is generally accepted, and it matters little whether we talk about longevity or quality of life, mental health or physical health, infectious diseases or chronic conditions – those lower down the ladder are just about always the worst off. It is no exaggeration, then, to say that class is a life-and-death issue.

It might be supposed that this is, or should be, less the case today than it once was, since we in the West now live in a world not only of affluence but of greater scientific knowledge, advanced medical techniques, government welfare and concerns for wellbeing. We are, after all, constantly being told what is good for us, what is bad for us, how much exercise we should do and so on – magazines, TV shows such as *You Are What You Eat*, films such as *Super Size Me* and official health campaigns are all in on the act, always citing the latest scientific findings on diet and exercise. These findings are, to be fair, constantly changing and contradicting each other, causing confusion and misunderstanding: one moment drinking wine is said to be healthy, the next it is to be avoided; beer is bad for us, then actually beer is good for us, then not again; we should do three half-hour stints of exercise a week because anything more is detrimental, then someone says we should do five bouts a week, or just frequent five-minute bursts, and so on. Yet this is still, according to some (e.g. Giddens, 1991), a new context of advice and choice, of information and plurality and of assessments of risk factors for this or that (heart disease, cancer etc.) which people of all classes must reflexively navigate in weaving together their lifestyle, even if its inconsistency can produce some anxiety. A boom in health foods has also occurred, with so-called 'superfoods' such as goji berries and probiotic drinks pushed on us, omega-3 oils injected into everything from milk to bread, supermarkets bringing out more healthy options, advertising based on how much calcium, wholegrain or cholesterol-busting properties an item has, and such like.

Yet none of this has reduced class inequalities. Certainly many of the old ailments and diseases that used to afflict the working class in pre-twentieth-century Western societies – malnutrition, scarlet fever, cholera, scrofula and so on, alongside industrial accidents and poor living and working conditions – have been cleared away or at least drastically reduced, and life expectancies have risen right across the board. However, in *relative* terms the differences in health and longevity are just as stark as ever, or in many respects even wider. Death rates per 100,000 for different age groups may well have fallen in all classes, for example, but they have fallen furthest in the top class; life expectancy has indeed crept up for all, but it has done so to a greater degree for the most advantaged; and general health and wellbeing may have improved, but this is disproportionately the case for those with most resources (Bartley, 2004; Dorling, 2013). A male routine manual worker in the UK is still statistically likely to die six years earlier than his higher manager/professional counterpart – and that number has increased since the early 1980s – while a female routine worker, despite having every

chance of spending longer on this earth than her male equivalent, is in all probability going to die four years earlier than
a female higher manager/professional of the same age (ONS,
2011). Depending on regions of residence, between a quarter
and a third of routine workers, moreover, whether male or
female, are likely to report being in poor health, compared
with around just 15 per cent of those in the top class (ONS,
2013) – and similar figures could be found for any other
Western nation (Graham, 2007).

Not only that, but the reasons for the higher mortality and
morbidity of the working class seem to have changed. No
longer is it a lack of food producing weak and malnourished
people, but an apparent excess of foods, and the wrong kind
of foods, producing obese people. There are still factors such
as poor housing with damp and pollution from nearby industrial areas, but now smoking and a lack of physical activity
have become more prominent in causing death and disease.
It seems as if some things have reversed – from feeble to fat,
from lack of food to excess of food, from excess of physical
labour to lack of physical labour – but the end result is still
the same.

How, then, have researchers tried to explain all this? If we
leave aside those who, on the basis of very little evidence,
brazenly claim that ill-health causes class position rather than
vice versa, how does class actually produce 'good' or 'bad'
health and different life expectancies? These are, to be honest,
questions that have slowly become quasi-monopolized by
epidemiologists or medical sociologists, with class researchers
generally engaging in these debates an awful lot less than they
used to and than they should – a consequence of increasing
specialization within sociology, no doubt – so the theories are
not necessarily the usual ones, at least in name. In this chapter,
however, I want to try to re-forge the links, review the key
theories offered or supported by health researchers, link them
back up to mainstream ideas about class and highlight what
they may be missing. In particular – and readers otherwise
inclined should be warned – I want to make the case that a
Bourdieusian approach to class integrates, repositions and
strengthens many of the themes and ideas espoused by others.
But let me begin with some of the most influential perspectives currently on the scene.

Materialism versus culturalism

For a long time when it came to explaining class inequalities in health there were really only two players in town: the 'materialist' approach and the 'cultural' approach. Both of them, like many things in this area, were first put on the map by a report published in the UK in 1980 called – after the name of the person who headed it – the Black Report (Townsend and Davidson, 1982). The authors had been commissioned by the Labour government of the late 1970s to examine the evidence for persisting inequalities and, along with charting the patterns, trends and international comparisons, they took it upon themselves to assess the leading ideas as to why the inequalities existed, pulling out materialism – sometimes also referred to as the 'structural' approach – and culturalism as the main contenders. The materialist explanation is fairly straightforward: lack of income to buy nutritional foods, lack of time and money to take up organized exercise, but also damp and uninsulated housing and pathogenic working conditions (because people do still labour physically, operate dangerous machinery and suffer the mental strains of having hard jobs) – things such as these constrain people and batter their minds and bodies without their knowing or being able to control it.

The authors of the report made no bones about the fact that they found this the most convincing explanation for health inequalities – and partly for that reason the report was effectively suppressed by the Conservative government when it was subsequently published on their watch, since it opposed their own views. No distinct theory of class underpins it, however. There was reference to Marxism in the report, as if it were synonymous with class analysis, and a rejoinder to the claim that capitalism has improved everyone's health and so cannot be the problem in the form of an argument that capitalism nevertheless inherently produces relative inequalities, but the measures of class and causal mechanisms discussed bore little resemblance to those that might be associated with Marxism. Perhaps the closest 'fit' is actually with a Weberian approach to class, since it might cohere with the logic of life chances – in the most literal sense – being shaped by income, work and housing, which are themselves the products of the market situation or employment relation that one finds oneself occupying. Indeed, some of the researchers involved in the project of turning Goldthorpe's class scheme into the NS-SEC were interested in doing so precisely in order to produce a better measure for studying health inequalities (see contributions to Rose and Pevalin, 2003).

The materialist approach, in its usual form, is fairly mechanical: people are forced and pressed to act in certain ways, and it seems to be assumed that everyone *would* buy healthy food, stop smoking and take up exercise – all believed to be inherently good things – if they suddenly had more money and time. Yet while health and longevity per se may be considered desirable, and therefore firmly under the rubric of life chances strictly defined, the goods and practices deemed appropriate means to those ends might well not be. Here we start to nudge towards the second explanation for health inequalities discussed by the Black Report: the 'culturalist' or 'behavioural' argument. There are, in fact, a few different versions of this line of thought, though all of them revolve around the idea that lifestyle choices or culture – defined in multiple ways – have some kind of impact on health behaviours (smoking, diet, exercise) autonomously from purely economic factors (Bartley, 2004). There are those who see it in terms of defective personalities – the working class have poor coping skills, suffer indecisiveness, are simply more prone to stress and so on – and those who see it in terms of uninformed or uneducated choices – the working class lack sense, information or, linking up with Peter Saunders' argument, the IQ to make the 'right' choices.

There are, however, more nuanced versions of this general idea, such as Cockerham's (2013) effort to link it up to Weber's ideas on status. Interestingly, since differences in health by ethnicity are, in Cockerham's view, attributable largely to class positions, we are talking specifically about social classes here, in Weber's sense, so the assumption must be that people develop certain customs of eating and activity or attitudes towards the body over time through common association and socialization, which then become differently valued. Weber himself, however, leaves the causal reasoning at interaction and never really broaches how and why certain behaviours linked to economic classes might be perpetuated as part of a social class, in the same way as, for example, the habitus as an adaptation to material conditions does for Bourdieu. Though we have already seen that there is an unclear connection between his definition of status and social classes, Goldthorpe, for his part, does posit a linking mechanism between status position and consumption, albeit one he has not applied directly to food – differential 'information processing capacity'; but this seems to land us in the territory of the cruder intelligence-based culturalist explanations.

The authors of the Black Report and others since have been sceptical about the power of cultural or behavioural explanations, but not so governments. Then and now, in the UK and elsewhere, health has generally been seen by politicians as a matter of individual lifestyle choice – usually on the basis of cruder versions of the behavioural model – and official strategies have frequently taken the form of public information campaigns designed to offer advice and tips on how to be healthy and encourage personal responsibility, pushing material circumstances off, or to the back of, the agenda (see Dorling, 2013). The big thing a few years ago in the UK and US, for example, was 'nudge theory', or the idea that people just needed little nudges here and there to jolt them out of their routinized ways of thinking about diet and so on, though like many fashionable ideas it soon receded from the political scene. In any case, some might go so far as to see this disjunction as an example of individualization, as described by Bauman (2001), in action: while material circumstances are the actual cause of ill-health, people are encouraged to see it purely in terms of their own free, individual actions and to keep up with the latest, transient information on what is best and what works, from exercising thirty minutes a day to the newest 'superfood', all of which keeps many companies in business.

The 'psychosocial' model: health gradients and status syndromes

Materialist and culturalist theories may have held court before and since the publication of the Black Report, but in recent times a third perspective has started to gain ground.

There are a few ways of describing it, with the label 'psycho-social' perhaps being the most popular, but the driving force behind it is a series of studies led by the epidemiologist Michael Marmot (for the overview see Marmot, 2004). Marmot and his team investigated the physical and mental health of civil servants of all ranks in Whitehall – the place where those involved in the administration of the UK central government work – and found something intriguing. Health inequalities were not distributed in a binary 'high-class versus low-class', 'routine workers versus professionals' kind of way. Instead, there was what they called a *health gradient*: at each and every step of the hierarchy, every grade of employment, no matter how small, there were progressive health inequalities. So the bottom of the ladder had the worst health, the next step up had better health, the next had better than them, and so on, until the top-grade administrators, who had the best health of all.

Crucially, Marmot and his team argued, these differences cannot be explained by material or cultural differences alone – those play a role, but not the key one here. After all, all of these workers were in white-collar jobs and avoided the hazards associated with manual work, and all of them were affluent enough to avoid poor living conditions and unhealthy foods. There were differences in lifestyle, to be sure, but in statistical terms cultural attributes such as diet and exercise seemed to explain very little.

So what was the cause of these health inequalities? Marmot concluded that if not material or cultural factors, or genetics for that matter, then hierarchical inequalities can only be explained by the very existence of hierarchy, or more precisely, the *psychosocial effects* of being in a hierarchy – whether of income, education or job grades. In other words, people lower down in the hierarchy with less control, autonomy and authority suffer all manner of negative psychological conditions precisely because they are lower down the hierarchy than others, such as stress, anxiety, low self-esteem, insecurity and so on. This can have two effects. It can lead people to drink and smoke to alleviate their woes, therefore increasing so-called risk-behaviours, but we know that is not that significant, says Marmot. More importantly, long-term biological stress can trigger depression, high blood pressure, high cholesterol, a weakened immune system and thus susceptibility to infection and all kinds of diseases. So, crucially, no matter how affluent society as a whole gets, as long as there is a hierarchy in some sense within it there will be inequality. The only way to tackle health inequalities would therefore seem to be to flatten the hierarchy somehow – notice the parallels with Goldthorpe on educational inequalities – but this is complicated by the fact that Marmot (2004) believes the existence of hierarchy to be a product of evolutionary psychology and instinct-driven struggles between men for females, who will automatically favour those with most resources to support their offspring.

That aside, the focus on relative inequalities has been taken further by Richard Wilkinson and Kate Pickett (2009) in their famous 'spirit level' thesis, though the attention shifts from trying to explain class disparities in health to demonstrating that *everyone* is less healthy in nations such as the US and UK where there are high income disparities. The logic is that the greater the level of income inequality in a society the more pronounced become status differences, the more intense therefore become struggles for status, and with that comes a greater risk of stress and anxiety and a decrease in health-sustaining social support and cooperation. As one might expect, Goldthorpe (2010) did not take too kindly to this apparent conflation of status with income – where the latter goes, the former follows – and pointed to historical instances where status struggles became more intense where income differences declined, since status is all that those who have lost out have left to make themselves stand out. He takes the opportunity to swipe at Bourdieu too, who he erroneously sees as saying the same sort of thing as Wilkinson and Pickett, but then goes on to support the conclusions reached by Torssander and Erikson (2010) that education – i.e. cultural capital – must be brought into the picture alongside economic factors such as class if we are to understand health inequalities fully.

The most dogged critics of the psychosocial approach, however, are those who champion what they call a 'neo-materialist' explanation of health (see especially Lynch et al., 2000, 2001, 2004; Muntaner and Lynch, 1999). They make three points. First, they reassert that health and ill-health are produced not by *perceptions* of inequality, as the psycho-social approach declares, but by the different material conditions that unequal resources afford. The famous analogy is with long-haul air travel. Passengers in first class have more room to sleep and nicer and more ample food, whereas those in economy class are cramped up and have lower-quality food. The former arrive at their destination refreshed and ready to go, while those from economy class feel hungry and haggard – the difference is not due to the people in economy class seeing those from first class and feeling anxious they were not like them, but the actual conditions their money bought them. How far that can be taken as an analogy for society is perhaps questionable, but a more down-to-earth example, so to speak, might be a damp and mouldy house, bought because it was cheap but too expensive to repair, producing ill-health through the spores it releases and *not* (generally) through a perception that the house is mouldier than someone else's.

The second point the neo-materialists make is that Wilkinson and Pickett focus too much on income inequality alone and neglect the wider material factors that can and do make a difference. They have in mind the level of state investment in welfare provision, healthcare services and educational systems, but also the strength of trade unions and women's participation in paid employment. Where investment, worker representation and gender equality are high in a nation it can offset the effects of income inequality, so the solution is to promote public spending and worker solidarity as well as reduce pay differentials. The neo-materialists also criticize the focus on social support, trust and community cohesion in the psychosocial approach, which come across as logical antidotes to status anxiety, since this can be harnessed to conservative, regressive agendas blaming the world's problems on lack of respect and fellow-feeling and seeking solutions in community self-help schemes.

Third, and most pertinently, the neo-materialists chide Wilkinson and Pickett for failing to provide any class-based political economic framework for understanding how inequalities in income come about in the first place. Pay differentials are simply taken as given and then assumed to be easily fixable without any consideration for the different interests that might underpin them. Muntaner and Lynch (1999) propose two remedies: first, to understand income differences between nations, we need to situate them within the global political economy using world-systems theory, since the core/periphery divide in the international division of labour is key; and second, we need to realize that income inequality is generated through *exploitation*. This is, in other words, a Marxist critique of the psychosocial model, with plenty of references to Wright, though the neo-materialists are rarely so explicit about their theoretical heritage.

The neo-materialists have generally concerned themselves with Wilkinson and Pickett and, therefore, with differences in average mortality and illness rates between nations rather than between classes within any one nation. But the style of their response raises a question: where are the Marxist interpretations of class-based health inequalities?

Marxism: social murder and greedy bastards

As it happens, one of the very first analyses of the connections between social conditions and health came from Marx's friend and collaborator, Friedrich Engels, in his inquiry into *The Condition of the Working Class in England* (1845/1987). After painstakingly documenting the abominable conditions of workers – their squalid housing, their hazardous neighbourhoods, their treacherous working conditions – and the catalogue of ailments suffered as a result – cholera, scrofula, typhoid, malnutrition and so on – he pointed the finger directly at the capitalist class. It was they who had impoverished the working class by paying the lowest possible wages, it was they who had produced the dank and toxic residences for the workers and their families to dwell in, and it was they who foisted back-breaking, bone-crunching, body-straining or simply life-ending working practices on the workers so as to maximize surplus value. Engels thus had no qualms in following the workers' movement of his day and declaring the unnecessary or early deaths among the proletariat 'social murder' – the bourgeoisie know, in some way, that these conditions are unlivable and cause death and disease, yet they insist on reproducing them in the service of capital accumulation.

It might be thought that Engels' diagnosis gradually lost its relevance through the twentieth century as the miseries of Victorian life were left behind and welfare regimes were put firmly in place. But later Marxists would disagree, prime among them Vincente Navarro (1976, 1978, 1986). He identified three major causes of ill-health among workers in the post-war capitalist West, all of which are produced inexorably by the socio-economic system: (1) industrial accidents and hazards, such as exposure to toxins, due to chronic underinvestment in health and safety by capitalists wanting to limit the costs of production as much as possible; (2) a lack of concern or action among capitalists for the noxious side effects of the production process on local communities (such as the emission of carcinogenic pollutants from factories); and most importantly of all (3) alienation at work, which produces mental health disorders and psychosomatic illnesses. This last process works in two ways, both of which might put Marmot's and Wilkinson's findings in a new light. First, alienation, being a lack of control over or connection to the process and product of one's labour, is inherently depressing and stressful since it counteracts the very essence of what it is to be human. Second, since employment is so alienating, workers are encouraged to find meaning in consumption instead – to define themselves by what they wear, drive and eat. This can spur precisely the kind of 'status syndrome' Marmot talks about, and thence further strain, but the fact that consumption needs are designed to be insatiable – because there will always be a new car, gadget or fashion one just has to have – brings its own health-damaging stresses and anxieties.

As if this was not enough, Navarro claims that even the development of public health programmes in the US and the National Health Service in the UK have served class interests. They may well have been in part a concession to the demands of the working class, i.e. a means of quelling rebellion, but in all cases they were designed specifically to meet the needs of the capitalist class, such as their relentless quest to commodify as much as possible, including products relating to treating and preventing ill-health, and the need to ensure alienation and industrialization did not make workers *unproductively* ill. And just to top it off, the whole field of medicine is not only controlled by members of the capitalist class (sitting on hospital boards and executive committees) but completely shot through with its ideology. It works, for example, with a notion of ill-health as something preventable and remediable through individual behaviour and therapy rather than social change, while Waitzkin (1983) has shown doctor–patient interactions and conversations revolve around the supposed 'expert' reinforcing the importance of getting back to work and assuaging anxieties.

However, after Navarro registered these ideas Marxism became rather less popular in medical sociology for familiar reasons: Foucault and the sociology of the body became the fashion, and while plenty of earnest analyses of class disparities continued, few – even the neo-materialists for the most part – ventured to encase them within an overarching sociological conception of class relations. The exception is Graham Scambler's (2002) purposively provocative 'greedy bastards hypothesis', or GBH, which basically updates things by claiming that health inequalities are the (mostly) unanticipated outcome of the top slice of capitalists pulling the levers of power in their favour, since they have engineered the huge income (or wealth) disparities and the 'de-standardization' of work (i.e. employment insecurity) shown by others to be at the root of so much physical and mental illness these days. Scambler is, however, a relatively lonely voice in medical sociology. On top of that, he has gone along with many of the criticisms of Marxism aired since Navarro started out – its economic reductionism, class reductionism and so on – and turned to the neo/post-Marxist Jürgen Habermas for inspiration instead of Marx directly. Since Habermas (1987) sidelines labour (and its exploitation) as the key to human existence and puts communication in its place, this leads Scambler to the view that the solution rests with social movements deepening dialogue and resisting expert power rather than any class-based revolution, but it also leaves more open than usual the question of why exactly these bastards are so damn greedy in the first place.

Bourdieu: bringing it all together

And so we come to the final perspective in understanding the link between social class and differences in mortality, morbidity and quality of life: the perspective of Bourdieu. To be honest Bourdieu is often pulled in to support different arguments at different times – Wilkinson and Pickett, for example, see their ideas as in tune with his, while Bartley (2004) herds him under the 'culturalist' label on account of the idea that health behaviours can be seen as part and parcel of the 'status striving' he apparently documents. These are not necessarily incorrect readings of Bourdieu, but they are partial ones, because the full logic of Bourdieu's take on class actually incorporates and reframes most of the arguments seen so far.

   The notion of conditions of existence, or relative distance from necessity, for example, incorporates a lot of what the materialists emphasize since these conditions set the limits of what is possible and impossible, affordable and off-bounds, preventing or allowing access to certain goods and practices, encased within the overall logic that this depends on the level of recognized resources, or capital, one possesses. Moreover, struggling to meet the demands of necessity – of paying bills and debts, of scraping money together for food, of going without and so on – can itself be a source of considerable mental strain. However, Bourdieu's real masterstroke came in providing a theoretical framework for grasping something which many health researchers since the days of the Black Report (e.g. Blaxter, 1992) had increasingly come to believe: that material factors and cultural factors are, in fact, thoroughly entwined (see Williams, 1995). The link is the habitus, as an adaptation to conditions of existence, or, more accurately, as the result of an effort to turn that which is attainable into a principle of recognition and value. The two key examples, both explored in *Distinction* (Bourdieu, 1984), are food and physical activity.

The food space and the space of sports

Everyone needs to eat to stay alive, but even the most cursory look at relevant evidence on who eats what quickly reveals stark differences in taste by class. Amongst the dominated, for instance, the financial and time demands of material necessity, plus high output of energy in hard jobs, mean that they tend to choose food that is cheap yet substantial, so fatty cuts of meat, potatoes, big steaming plates of pasta in quick-and-easy sauces, stuff to 'keep you going', 'fill you up', 'fill a hole' – certainly nothing too 'fiddly' or 'finicky' such as fish with bones in it. On top of that is the dominated orientation towards time and the body: dealing with the demands of necessity anchors people in the present and near future, cap-tured in phrases such as 'taking life as it comes', 'enjoying the moment', 'living for the day' and so on, which leads at one and the same time to a desire for what Bourdieu called 'convivial indulgence' – a lack of constraint or reticence in eating or drinking together, 'having a laugh', enjoying oneself and so on, with no airs or graces – and concerning oneself little with the health content of the food (its saltiness, sugari-ness or fattiness), since the taste in the present is valued more than some abstract assessment of its probable impact on a distant bodily future.

In the petite bourgeoisie above them, however, we see a different orientation. The petit bourgeois is, in Bourdieu's phrase, the person who tries to make themselves small to become bourgeois – in other words, accumulating capital by cutting back, saving, valuing sobriety, modesty, decency and so on – and this plays out in food tastes as much as anything else. In the cultural capital-rich fraction of the petite bour-geoisie, where budgets are tight but obscure knowledge ampler, they also value foods which their resources make available, namely the exotic, the original, the 'kooky', the experimental or 'different' but not necessarily the expensive – maybe Vietnamese or Korean cuisine, spinach smoothies or green tea.

And then we get to the dominant class. At the pole where economic capital is plentiful and the hedonistic lifestyle rules, we see a taste for exclusive cuisine with rare and expensive ingredients, an orientation towards maximization of sensual pleasure, much as in the dominated class, but with a focus on lightness and refinedness (caviar and truffles), effort and technique (lobster, oysters, bony fish) and ostentatious pres-entation because no pressure to feed oneself and fill up one's family is felt here. A more distanced and playful approach to food can thus develop – so everything that we might think of as haute cuisine, fine dining, Michelin star restaurants and such like. Within the cultural fraction of the dominant class, on the other hand, there is a mastery of abstract ideas about health and the body and a longer-term orientation towards the future allowed by the security their resources afford them, allowing them to conceive of their body as a project to be worked on through sacrifice of immediate satisfactions. Here is where we get, amongst other things, a concern for healthy, lean, 'natural' foods, such as raw vegetables, grilled or poached meats, couscous and bulgar wheat and yoghurt and fruit for pudding. Of course these are *tendencies* that blur into one another in different parts of the social space. The actual manifestation of these tastes in any one concrete person's life will depend on, amongst other things (not least their gender and ethnicity), their precise position and – converging a little with the growing interest in health research in the effects of changes over the 'life course' – trajectory through social space, as well as the state of supply provided by food manufacturers and distributors contending within the economic field.

Bourdieu applies the same logic to sport and exercise. In some cases we can see associations of particular activities with particular sections of the social space, but in other cases what matters might be the different ways in which people from different classes approach the same activity. In the dominated section of social space, where the body is often put to hard or tiring use at work, there is often little inclination to batter it further with exercise, and where sports are taken up they tend to be ones that put an emphasis on brute *strength* and explosive exertion of energy – as a form of physical capital – but also *docility* (in the form of either commitment to the team, collective discipline, or submission to the drilling of a trainer, as in boxing) and *competition*, premised on an instrumental approach to the body as a means to an immediate, or near, satisfying end, i.e. winning, or the 'buzz' of taking part.

Higher up in social space, we see amongst the economic fractions of the dominant class (and of the intermediate class to a lesser extent) a taste for sports demanding high economic investment but low physical exertion, the emphasis being more on a skill in relation to particular apparatus (yachting, horse riding, golfing, skiing), while amongst the cultural fraction of the dominant class physical activity is woven into a long-term conception of the body as an end in itself – again a project of development through sacrifice, oriented by abstract goals and ideas about the body (calories, energy, muscle groups) and often undertaken in solitude as a form of self-directed mental discipline (jogging, yoga, tai chi). At the cultural pole of the petite bourgeoisie, finally, due to the same disposition to maximize recognition with the resources they have that we saw with food, there is often a focus on new, funky, unusual sports (snowboarding, 'speedminton' etc.) as well as a concern with appearance and liberation (gymnastics).

Overall, just as lifestyles in general form a symbolic space homologous with the social space and acting as markers of people's positions, so we can distinguish a specific 'food space' and 'space of sports' with the same key differentiating principles – manner versus matter, form versus function, substance versus style – mapping over the class structure. Obviously Bourdieu's own evidence related to France in the 1960s and 1970s, but many researchers have more or less confirmed and updated the general structure and underlying dispositions of the spaces in different countries at different times and with different methods, albeit not always with the best measures of class (see e.g. Tomlinson, 1998; Vandebroeck, 2013; Veenstra, 2007; Wills et al., 2011; Atkinson and Deeming, forthcoming). To dwell on just one example, Mike Savage and his colleagues (1992) anglicized Bourdieu's argument by looking at lots of statistical data on lifestyle practices and social position in Britain. They found that within what they call 'the middle class' there was a section that was ultra-healthy, doing plenty of exercise such as jogging and yoga and eating healthy foods. This healthy section had far more cultural capital than economic, and tended to be teachers, social workers, and people in medical occupations. More towards the economic pole this healthiness was much less pronounced, and in the middle there was a curious mix of ultra-healthiness and ultra-hedonism, so faddy diets and exercise regimes mixed with binge-drinking and unhealthy food – people who are, in short, living contradictions.

Charting the patterns and dispositions is only part of the story, however. For Bourdieu the whole point of uncovering these differences and their relationship to class was to uncover which lifestyles are deemed more legitimate, which win more recognition on a broad scale – or *mis*recognition since there is nothing *intrinsically* more valuable about them – and which are automatically denigrated in the process. This puts the whole focus on healthy eating in government and media campaigns, and those who would criticize the dietary or exercise habits of people with fewer resources than them (as 'greedy', 'stupid' or 'lazy'), in a new light. For what is this if not a clear example of *symbolic violence*, the pushing on to the dominated of the dominant way of life, grounded in certain conditions of existence and, ultimately, arbitrary – is there anything *inherently* better about self-denying in the quest to live as long as possible rather than enjoying the moment? – as the universally legitimate one which everyone should aspire to no matter what their own conditions of life. Bourdieu himself was of the view that eating was one of the few areas in which the working class could mount a strong challenge to the dominant mode of living, but perhaps things have changed now that, amongst other things, reality television programmes constantly parade members of the dominated class as shameful in their culinary habits while an 'expert' rich in all kinds of capital doles out tips on how they can be 'better people' (Skeggs and Wood, 2011). Certainly that would explain why research reveals a sense of guilt or shame when these standards cannot be lived up to, or an effort to define one's own way of life as 'healthy' in its own way – making sure children are getting fed rather than going without, for example (e.g. Atkinson, 2012b; Atkinson and Bradley, 2013).

The impact of struggles in the field of power

I stated that Bourdieu can integrate much of what other theories of health inequalities pinpoint as the key, but so far only a synthesis of materialist and culturalist arguments has been offered. How, then, to bring Marmot's studies and Marxism into the mix? In a nutshell, both, it seems to me, are perhaps best approached through the notion of the field of power. In Marmot's case, since the target population was everyone working in Whitehall, the home of the British civil service, it could be that what he is finding is less about class directly than about what Bourdieu called the *bureaucratic field*, i.e. the state as a field of struggle, with its own dominant and dominated factions defined by their possession of the specific forms of capital valued there, and that any 'psychosocial' effects detected apparently distinct from material/cultural factors may well ultimately issue from the struggle for, and lack of, recognition *within that field*, even if Marmot's uni-dimensional measure of inequality probably hides the full picture of difference. The same logic might equally apply to other fields, such as acting (since Marmot points out those with more awards and thus 'higher' in the field tend to live longer than those with few or none), opening up possibilities for a research agenda into the specific physical and mental health effects of recognition struggles.

As for Marxism, whether it be capitalist underinvestment in workplace safety, production of toxic or otherwise unhealthy products or 'greedy bastards' heightening job inse-curity and disparities in distance from necessity, it is not hard – despite what Bourdieu's old-guard critics might argue – to locate the processes fingered in terms of the economically rich fraction of the dominant class, through its struggles in the economic field, seeking to maximize their interests and their resources. Filling in the gaps for Scambler, however, we embed that insight within an understanding that those interests are no less a product of the struggle for recognition than any other interest, just ones that indicate the immense value of money in capitalist society as a – if not the overriding – prin-ciple of symbolic worth.

Conclusion

The two key messages of this chapter are fairly similar to the ones seen for social mobility and educational inequalities. First of all, there have indeed been distinct changes in the

nature of class inequalities over the years, with shifts in absolute death rates, chances of suffering certain diseases and life
expectancy for all – matching shifts in absolute rates of mobility and educational take-up – but the *relative* differences
produced by the persisting class structure are, once again, as
stark as ever, if not starker. Discussions of everyone living
longer than ever and the ensuing problems of an 'ageing
population', even with the standard acknowledgement of
gender differences, therefore rather mask the fact that the
chances of getting to a ripe old age, and doing so in relatively
good condition, are not the same for a lawyer and a labourer,
whether male or female. The second message is that the best
explanation of health inequalities, as with social immobility
and educational inequality, lies in a conceptualization of class
that refuses to separate the material from the cultural, or the
economic from the symbolic, or, put crudely, money from
education, and to focus only on the first in each case. Just
as economic capital *and* cultural capital (along with social
capital) help us make sense of social mobility and explain
educational pathways, so too they are both crucial to understanding the way in which so-called 'health behaviours' are
woven into a whole modus vivendi, or class ethos, and how
apparently benevolent government drives to increase population health, as they stand, are implicated in the ceaseless,
unequal battle to define and impose the right way to live.

9
Politics and Identity

'Politics' and 'identity' are not just about who someone wants to vote for in an election, whether they are a member of a particular party or which pre-defined categories they think they might fit into on a survey. 'Politics' is about what people consider right, just, proper or valuable in life – perhaps lofty ideals such as freedom, equality or environmental protection, or maybe just something that they believe would make their daily existence that little bit easier, such as lower taxes or better public services (the local buses, hospital, schools), affordable childcare and unpolluted rivers. It is also, of course, a case of asserting that what others believe and value is wrong – that others are 'looking after themselves', 'wanting handouts' or whatever – and that might be in relation to everyday concerns or principles of political philosophy. 'Identity', on the other hand, is about what makes us feel different from or similar to others, what we believe unites and separates us, where or with whom we think we 'belong', how we describe ourselves and each other and, inevitably, how we attack and belittle each other in the struggle to justify our own place in the world.

Sometimes politics and identity come together. People not only get passionate about their values or demands and want to act, sometimes violently, to assert or defend them, but join together with people they consider to be in a similar situation and with similar interests to do so, from peasants revolting against feudal lords and factory workers striking and rioting over their work conditions to the worldwide uprisings of May 1968 initiated by left-leaning students and contemporary campaigns against government cuts. This is the bread and butter of Marxist historiography, Weberian notions of class formation and Bourdieu's ideas about group-making, though it must be remembered that not every conjunction of identity with political action is obviously about class, even if it often comes into the picture somewhere – one thinks, for example, of the suffragette movement, which, while drawing in women from across the class structure, was undoubtedly led by well-to-do women.

An argument today, however, is that while class may well have been a driving force in politics in the past and a key component of how people saw themselves, and the world in general, this is no longer the case. Political issues which have absolutely nothing to do with class, from animal rights and environmentalism to multiculturalism and immigration, now dominate the agenda, the claims go, and identities in the twenty-first century revolve around anything but class – ethnicity, nationality, religion, gender, sexuality, choice of clothes and music and so on. So how have class researchers responded to this? Have they accepted a decline in the political and subjective significance of their chosen topic or fought back in some way? Does it differ depending on the definition of class that they adhere to?

All these questions and more are the subject of this chapter. After having outlined the trends and changes which gave rise to the challenge to class I will indicate some of the ways in which Marxists, Weberians and Bourdieusians have responded, making the case in particular that the last of these offer a fresh and encompassing perspective by distinguishing between 'class' politics and identities on the one hand, where values and perceptions are explicitly articulated with the language of class, and *classed* politics and identities on the other, wherein 'class' as a label may be absent but attitudes towards all manner of issues and orientations to self and others still remain anchored within the divisions of social space. First, however, I want to lay out some socio-historical background, tracing the 'way the world was' in the West up until about the 1960s, because it was during this time that class politics and identities were apparently at their peak.

Class politics and class identities

With capitalism's emergence, and the transformation of feudal peasants into paid labourers, three particular developments were key to the consolidation of a general sense that politics and society were fractured along lines of 'class', however that term might have been understood. The first was the establishment in the US and Europe of trade unions in the early nineteenth century, initially as fairly clandestine organizations but then eventually with legal recognition. Up until then workers had been expressing their frustration with their meagre pay and punishing working conditions largely through violent and haphazard revolts and riots. These were usually swiftly repressed and denounced by factory owners, politicians and others. With unions, however, grievances could be knitted together into a general notion – regional, national or beyond – of 'the workers' lot' and members presented as a bloc, with a unified interest opposed to the unified interests of an antagonist (capitalists), and, drawing on the emerging discourses of the day (including that promulgated by Marx), described in terms of one 'class' versus another. The leaders of the unions thus claimed to be able to speak and fight in the name of this thing called 'the working class', and increasingly sought to do so not through the simple smashing of machinery (or heads) but through orchestrated strikes and demonstrations, hitting capitalists where it hurt most – the pocket.

The second development was the extension of the right to vote in general elections to non-propertied (male) citizens, brought in between the late nineteenth and early twentieth centuries in most Western countries. The results were as might be expected: soon enough parties claiming to represent the workers' interests sprang up and gained electoral ground, championing the causes of equality, higher taxes and public ownership of industry – or, in a word, socialism – but via the ballot box and peaceful implementation rather than violent revolution. Aristocrats and business owners, on the other hand, who had once been the two warring parties in political matters, unified their interests in opposition, generally favouring free markets as well as traditional social relationships. This led to a situation of so-called 'alignment' (see e.g. Lipset and Rokkan, 1967), in so far as class positions now matched up very closely with both political viewpoints and parties – workers with the left, owners and managers with the right. There were variations in its strength between countries, depending largely on whether a country was generally Catholic, and therefore able to attract working-class voters to the right, or Protestant in orientation, and in some particularly rural areas one could still find a certain amount of 'deference voting', where workers voted for the right because they believed their masters to be socially superior to them, but the general trend across the developed world was one of growing alignment.

The emergence of trade unions and workers' parties were both said to have brought about a 'democratization' or 'institutionalization' of class conflict by the mid-twentieth century (Dahrendorf, 1959; Lipset, 1960). Conflict between workers and owners (or the managers they employed) was fought out no longer directly and chaotically on the streets but through formal, institutional channels, with representatives of each side, whether union leaders and company personnel or members of opposed parties, arguing over a table, or before parliament, and negotiating and bargaining over outcomes – better pay here, improved conditions there, more investment in public services, but not so much as to upset the applecart, and so on. The consequence of this was a decline of radicalism: instead of arguing for an overthrow of the system, the workers became a *part* of the system and pursued increasingly small-scale issues of pay and conditions through democratic debate and standardized procedures, and most workers felt less need to take action themselves because they believed someone had been delegated to do that for them. The situation was summed up by Michael Mann (1973), who famously claimed there are four essential features to the kind of revolutionary working-class consciousness posited by Marxists – a sense of shared identity on the basis of place in the productive process, a sense of opposition to another class, a belief that class is the all-encompassing feature of life and the envisioning of an alternative society – but that while the first two might have been common enough the latter two were too often scuppered by in-fighting and a mindset more concerned with piecemeal reform than sweeping change.

The third development, a product of capitalist development, was that workers from the countryside had been brought to the cities and concentrated in particular neighbourhoods and towns built around factories, mines, docks and such like. There was little social and geographical mobility away from them, so families tended to stay within these communities over generations. Neighbourhoods thus became relatively homogeneous, everyone knew everyone through work or family ties, they identified with one another and knew themselves to be different from bosses or the professionals (doctors, lawyers, churchmen) who entered their worlds briefly, using the language of 'us and them', 'our superiors' and so on to make sense of it all. An enormous amount of research was done in the UK on these communities, generally from an anthropological point of view since sociology was still young, but research in the US also documented how small towns were essentially partitioned along class lines (Lynd and Lynd, 1929). Some of the classics include Bott (1971), Dennis et al. (1969), Hoggart (1957), Stacey (1960) and Young and Willmott (1962).

With hindsight, and later historical research, the general view is that these community studies tended to exaggerate homogeneity and internal unity, romanticizing working-class ways of life which they thought were under threat and ignoring gender oppression and rival factions within the working class on the basis of skill, occupation or industry (Crow and Allen, 1994). We might instead think of these communities as local social spaces in the sense described in chapter 4, riven with internal struggles and divisions at the same time as being united by certain orientations and assumptions. In any case, the general view is that class politics and class identity were at their height by the mid-twentieth century, and that the very notion of 'class' itself was frequently used to frame conflicts and interests.

The decline of 'class'?

From the 1950s and 1960s onwards things began to change. First came the argument that increased affluence and contentment among the working class had brought about a more 'privatistic' orientation – workers treated their jobs as means to an end (money for buying consumer goods) rather than all-encompassing, they focused more on their home life and family leisure than socializing with workmates or others in the community, and they tended to see the world not in terms of 'us versus them' any more but as a simple case of 'rich versus poor'. The classic statement of this came from David Lockwood (1966), but a lot of the community studies scholars had also noticed the trend and seen it as a danger to the way of life they documented.

More drastic changes and arguments were to come, however. In the 1970s, for example, there emerged the influential idea that in prosperous post-industrial societies, where poverty and the needs of hunger, health and opportunity were essentially taken care of, material concerns and divisions were receding into the background and a collection of new 'post-materialist' issues – concerns over the environment, nuclear power, family values, religious freedom and so on – coming to the fore, and, since these had nothing to do with class, stances on them stubbornly refused to match up with class positions in any neat and straightforward way. Ronald Inglehart (1977) was the first to push this idea, but in more recent years Giddens (1991) also claimed that the 'emancipatory' politics associated with class struggle were giving way to a new era of 'life politics' revolving around lifestyle concerns – abortion, animal rights, environmentalism, peace, sexuality and so on – and others heralded the rise of 'identity politics', in which recognition for and acceptance of religious, ethnic or sexual differences became the prime demand (Calhoun, 1994).

Since traditional political parties struggled to keep up with or make space for these changing concerns, moreover, the very way in which post-materialist politics are conducted and the agents who struggle over them bear little resemblance to those of the days of old. Instead of unions and workers versus bosses and big business fighting through mainstream party politics, we have a whole range of 'new social movements' (NSMs) – pressure groups and organizations (e.g. Greenpeace, Amnesty International, animal rights groups and so on) formed by a mix of people, usually fairly well-educated, campaigning on single issues outside of mainstream politics through demonstrations, campaigns and rallies. The key theorists of this move include Melucci (1980), Habermas (1981) and Offe (1985).

These developments were later compounded by the rise of neoliberalism, a doctrine utterly opposed to notions of 'class' and class-based politics. The 1980s in particular was a decade of relentless assault from neoliberals, most famously Britain's own prime minister at the time, Margaret Thatcher. She closed down the mines and docks in droves in order to redirect the economy towards financial services, passed legislation to decimate the powers of unions, exhorted people to be entrepreneurial – to 'look after number one' – and claimed not only that society did not exist (only individuals and families did), at the same time as appealing to nationalist sentiments through the Falklands war, but that 'class' itself was a 'communist concept' and should be banished from political talk altogether.

Yet neoliberal ideas, anti-union policies and individualist language were not just confined to conservatives such as Thatcher or her US counterpart, Ronald Reagan, but managed to find a home among the parties that had originally been set up to protect workers' interests too, whether the Socialists in France, Labor in Australia, the Democrats under Clinton in the US or 'New' Labour in the UK. Socialist ideals were expunged from manifestos, privatization and free markets were embraced in a bid to woo increasingly affluent workers and the business vote, and explicit talk of class was openly disavowed, with New Labour's Tony Blair, for instance, announcing his party sought to move beyond a discourse of 'bosses versus workers' or 'middle class versus working class'. All this marginalized those who remained on the left and rendered much of the poorer working class without any meaningful representation at all, save from far-right nationalist parties myopically blaming the lack of jobs and houses produced by deindustrialization and state retrenchment on immigrants.

As a consequence of all this the three foundation stones of 'class' politics and identities laid during the eighteenth and nineteenth centuries seemed to have been turned upside down. Trade union membership – usually measured as 'union density', or the percentage of the workforce signed up to a trade union – has been declining in most Western nations for the past few decades, save in a few select countries, thus weakening the major mouthpiece of 'the working class' and advocate of class-based politics (figure 9.1). We have, more-over, apparently witnessed a steady process of 'dealignment', with class position having less and less bearing on which party people want to vote for (Sarlvik and Crewe, 1983; Clark and Lipset, 2001). Highly paid and highly educated professionals are increasingly tending to vote left while the working class embrace Conservatism and the far right, and not just because of stances on post-materialist issues but because of views on materialist ones such as redistribution and public ownership too. A common way of demonstrating this is by charting changes in the 'Alford index', which is worked out by subtracting from the proportion of manual workers voting left the proportion of non-manual workers

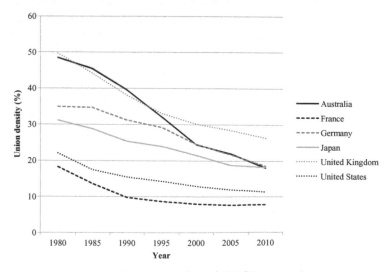

Figure 9.1   Union density in selected OECD countries
Source: OECD statistics, http://stats.oecd.org

voting left. For example, if 70 per cent of manual workers vote left and only 30 per cent of non-manual workers do, the index score is 40, which is quite high, but if 50 per cent of manual workers vote left and 40 per cent of non-manual workers vote left then we get an index score of 10, which is particularly low. In most Western countries the index score plummeted by half between the 1960s and the 1980s, dropping from 46 to 34 in Sweden, 42 to 21 in the UK, 26 to 10 in Germany, 20 to 14 in France and 18 to 8 in the US (Pakulski and Waters, 1996: 134).

Finally, bound up with all that has been said so far, but also thanks to social and geographical mobility in the wake of occupational change and expanding education systems, deindustrialization ripping the adhesive core out of local communities, globalization bringing waves of migrants into working-class areas and consumerism allowing new ways to define ourselves however we like, identification with a 'class', or even just talking about 'class' and seeing the world in those terms, is often said to have declined too. Without a doubt the key figures making that kind of claim are Beck (1992), Bauman (2001) and Giddens (1991), the theorists of individualization and reflexivity we saw in the opening chapter.

Marxist and Weberian responses

So what has been the reaction within the class analysis community to all this? We have already seen at various points, first of all, that many a high-profile Marxist, from Laclau and Mouffe to Habermas, responded fairly dramatically by more or less accepting (or even contributing to) the analysis and abandoning interest in class, largely because political action was so central to the very nature and point of class for them. Among those who have kept faith, however, probably the most elaborate and focused study of class consciousness and class politics in recent times came from Erik Olin Wright (1997). Starting out from his own particular way of seeing the link between class position and consciousness – as an individual phenomenon, worked out in response to the limits of the person's situation, rather than a collective entity, and as contingent, probable and in competition with other identities and conflicts rather than inevitable and primary – Wright proceeded by constructing a scale of 'anti-capitalist' views running from +10 (very anti-capitalist) to −10 (very pro-capitalist) and seeing where the incumbents of all the different class locations in his second scheme typically sat on it. He then compared scores across three countries: the US, Sweden and Japan.

However, while he certainly did find that workers tend to be more anti-capitalist on his scale than the bourgeoisie and the middle class in all three countries, Wright's analysis was hardly a convincing confirmation of class's centrality to the political landscape. He himself was puzzled by the stark and unusual differences between nations – in Japan, for example, *all* classes were more on the anti-capitalist side of the scale, with the petite bourgeoisie the most anti-capitalist of all – and chalked it up to the specific institutions and political histories of each. More importantly he completely ignored post- (or non-)materialist politics, or even broader materialist attitudes pertaining to life chances, even though these may actually be far more important to people and shape their political action (Marshall et al., 1988). Using a scale also rather papers over possible differences in responses to each question included – somebody utterly opposed to strikes but in favour of public ownership might get the same score as someone utterly opposed to public ownership but in favour of strikes, for example, yet those stances might vary by class position (Gerteis and Savage, 1998). Perhaps most tellingly, however, despite the fact that Wright seems to have come up with an incredibly narrow and simplistic measure of the link between class and politics, he himself admitted that class explains only a fairly small percentage of total variation in pro/anti-capitalist values (Wright, 1996) and, later, that class does indeed seem to be a weakening political force (Wright, 2010).

As for the Weberians, their response to the challenges to class has been threefold. First, they respond to Inglehart by recasting the 'post-materialist' issues he spotlights as a question of liberalism versus authoritarianism: being against nuclear weapons and the death penalty, pro-choice on abortion, in favour of immigration and such like makes one 'liberal' and having the opposite views makes one an 'authoritarian'

(Heath et al., 1985). This is then seen as separable from the traditional left–right continuum on materialist issues and, unlike the latter, is found to correspond not to class, as defined by the Nuffield School, but to *education* – actually a point made long ago by Lipset (1960). Goldthorpe (1999) himself is of the view that this is one of those differences that concerns situs, but research stubbornly shows that education is the crux: the higher one's education, the more liberal one is (Houtman, 2003). In any case, the Nuffield School seem to accept the rise of post-materialist or non-materialist issues, but since they are held not to correspond to class in any straightforward way this could amount to a tacit acceptance that class is a weaker force in politics than it once was.

Second, when it comes to the alignment between class and voting the Weberians make a few points. For a start, the Alford index has to go: its binary division of manual/non-manual work is just too crude a measure of class, unable to account, for example, for the particularly pro-market and low-tax approach of the petite bourgeoisie who may still technically be manual workers (self-employed plumbers, builders and so on). It also focuses on absolute levels of voting, but as with most things what matter for the Nuffield School are the relative rates – not how many working-class people vote for Labour and how many middle-class people for the Conservatives, that is, but the relative odds of a working-class person voting Labour compared to a middle-class person. Once we use the EGP scheme, and examine relative rates, and if we take a longer-term view – many of the dealignment claims in Britain, for instance, start from the general election of 1964, a particular high point in class alignment, meaning anything after that is bound to look like dealignment – a rather different trend in voting emerges. In fact the trend is, paradoxically enough, but reminiscently of the 'constant flux' argument on social mobility, one of 'trendless fluctuation': ups and downs from election to election in the extent of alignment with no clear overall direction (Heath et al., 1985; Evans, 1999). This has nothing to do with the strength of class over time, since differences in views on materialist issues tend not to change that much (Evans, 1993), but simply reflects the state of the political scene come election time – what policies are being offered, how effective or reliable the parties are considered to be and so on. This even led Goldthorpe (1999) to make the claim that transformations in the relationship between classes and parties were not for sociology to explain, let alone class analysis, but are a political issue with their own autonomy.

In more recent work, however, members of the Nuffield School have admitted that the trend has turned more towards steady dealignment, but they have sought to explain this through changes in the shape of the class structure – specifically the shrinkage of the working class – and the efforts of political parties to readapt their ideological stances in the wake of this, with left-leaning parties abandoning the remaining working class and moving to the right in order to stay electable (Evans and Tilley, 2012). Added to this, however, has to be the increasing awareness that since liberalism, and with that a vote for the left, is related to education, the 'service class', far from being more or less conservative, as Goldthorpe generally assumes, is bisected into a left-liberal, highly educated fraction and a less educated yet still affluent right-wing fraction made up of managers and business owners (see, for example, contributions to Evans, 1999).

Finally, there is the question of class identity. For a long time the debate here was structured around the research of Marshall et al. (1988), a defence of the strength of class identity which caused some stir because of the way the research was done. A more recent contribution, however, comes from Heath et al. (2010), who have studied patterns in the degree to which people identify with a class, and feel a sense of belonging to that class, from the 1960s up to the twenty-first century in Britain. The findings, in short, are (1) the number of people readily identifying with a class is relatively low, at between 40 and 50 per cent, but that is no different from the past and shows (surprise, surprise) no consistent trend over time; (2) there has been a change, however, in which class people identify with, as more people, no matter what their jobs, tend to identify as middle class than working class these days – no doubt, so the reasoning goes, because of changes in the class structure and the effects of social mobility; (3) there has also been a noticeable decline in the degree to which people feel 'close to' other people within their class; (4) and finally, there is some increasing 'looseness' in class identity, with more middle-class people claiming to be working-class and vice versa.

All three responses of the Nuffield School, however, are problematic. The two points on politics demonstrate the 'attenuation' of class and class analysis in their hands that we saw in chapter 3. Only because they cleave education and culture from class, for example, does the liberal–authoritarian axis of political stances become tricky for class analysis by overshadowing 'real' class politics and bifurcating the top class. Abandoning analysis of the changing political scene to political science, moreover, neglects the way that political strategies and policy programmes are themselves often the product of struggles between people from different classes and class fractions *within* the world of politics – political wrangles are only ever *relatively* autonomous from class, as well as gendered and ethnic interests, of course. And finally the whole approach of asking people to identify with one of two pre-given class categories is limited, overlooking the divergent meanings people might give to the different labels, ignoring the ways in which people develop and adapt their own labels for making sense of their place in the world and presupposing that historically specific categories will and should be relevant – indeed *imposing* them as relevant in the very questions themselves.

These problems can be circumvented, and indeed people have increasingly been trying to circumvent them, by turning for inspiration to Bourdieu instead. With this move, what becomes clear is not a decline of class but, instead, a distinction between explicit 'class' politics and implicit *classed* politics, and between explicit 'class' identities and *classed* identities.

Classed politics and identities

Bourdieu's (1984) own view on the relationship between class and politics is actually fairly complex, factoring in the different degree to which people feel they have a 'right to speak' (demonstrated in the higher proportion of the dominated class answering 'don't know' when polled on political issues), the different 'modes of production' of opinion (opposing those who toe the party line and those rich in cultural capital who seek to formulate an 'independent' view) and a difference between views on 'political order' – i.e. materialist issues – and views on 'moral order' – i.e. issues of liberalism/authoritarianism. He also talks in one place about a distinct 'field of labour struggle' (Bourdieu, 1993). We can, however, distil the following key points from Bourdieu's stance. First, just as we can map out differences in lifestyle, including food and sport, and examine their correspondence to positions in the social space of classes, we can map out a space of political views, values and inclinations – or political position-takings, as Bourdieu put it – and investigate the homology with class positions. Bourdieu himself, on the basis of a relatively limited analysis, was of the view that there was one axis opposing those leaning left (the dominated) and those leaning right (the economically rich) and another axis opposing those with extreme views (communist manual workers and economically liberal industrialists) and those with more moderate or apathetic views (those richer in cultural capital). More recent work by Harrits et al. (2010) in Denmark, however, has examined the distribution of a wide range of political position-takings – not just those that are explicitly and historically to do with 'class' – and found the space to be structured in the manner shown in figure 9.2 (cf. also Rosenlund, 2009).

Just as those who go to museums often are more likely to go to art galleries and read books when we look at lifestyles, so those against nuclear weapons and censorship are also more likely to be for gay rights and free speech, those favouring punitive measures on law and order are more likely to be in favour of traditional values on family and strict immigration, those favouring low taxes are more likely to be in favour of privatization and those supporting strong trade unions are more likely to be in favour of wealth redistribution. In other words, the views coalesce and cluster into four quadrants of liberalism, authoritarianism, pro-capitalism and socialism.

When we check the homology with the social space, what we see is that while materialist values correspond to volume of capital, forming a diagonal opposing the dominant and the dominated, the liberal–authoritarian opposition is a phenomenon of capital composition, the second axis of the social

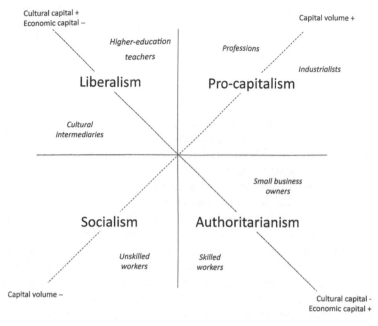

Figure 9.2 The homology between the social space and space of political position-takings

space. Since political parties tend to court the electorate on both issues to different degrees, the tendency to vote left or right therefore does not follow a binary split of manual/non-manual workers, or the working class versus the service class, but instead opposes the dominated class *and* those rich in cultural capital, on the one hand, to those richest in capital and richest in economic capital in particular on the other. This may well register as dealignment with the simplistic Alford index, and may well get EGP scheme users scratching their heads since it cuts through their classes in an unanticipated way, but adopting Bourdieu's multidimensional vision of class thus allows us to see that even the newer issues not traditionally bound up with what are historically seen as 'class politics' correspond to class positions and therefore remain *classed*.

The relationship between volume of capital and economic attitudes might seem relatively straightforward – people's views are oriented towards whatever is going to maintain or improve their possession of recognized resources. The nature of the link between education (or cultural capital) and liberalism, on the other hand, is rather more contentious. Bourdieu himself offers few helpful pointers here, but we might conjecture that it comes down in part to the opposition between symbolic mastery, or the tendency to locate experience and interests within abstract languages and conceptualizations of how the world works, and practical mastery, the mode of knowing the world oriented towards 'getting things done' in the most pragmatic and efficient way. We have to be careful not to lapse into dispensing symbolic violence here by construing practical mastery, which is attuned to particular conditions of existence after all, as simply 'stupidity' or lack of 'sophistication' as Lipset (1960) did and many people from the dominant class might do. Also important, however, might be the channelling of symbolic mastery in certain directions. Research consistently shows that the liberalism–education link is mediated heavily by the specific subject(s) studied: humanities and arts make one more liberal, since they demand and develop a symbolic mastery, and fundamental questioning of the 'naturalness', of social and human affairs, whereas business, management studies, law and engineering take the social world as it is and even serve to maintain it (Van de Werfhorst and de Graaf, 2004; Stubager, 2008; cf. Bourdieu, 1988). Since the former tend to be taken up at an increasingly disproportionate rate by women and the latter by men, no doubt there is a gendered dimension to this too.

Notice that, since the liberal–authoritarian axis encompasses many of the so-called post-materialist issues motivating most NSMs, this somewhat debunks their supposed 'classless' character. Instead it might simply be that, since the mainstream parties in most Western nations still primarily address – or are associated in people's minds with addressing – materialist issues, those who are most liberal or authoritarian, but more centrist on many materialist issues – namely the cultural (new) and economic (old) wings of the petite bourgeoisie, i.e. media/social service workers and small businesspeople respectively – have looked for a means, and mobilized their resources, to promote their interests outside of the usual channels. The ecology movement, for example, has been located by Klaus Eder (1993) squarely among the new petite bourgeoisie, and the same sort of logic can be extended to campaign groups addressed to abortion, nuclear weapons or nationalist sentiment.

A second way in which Bourdieu allows for added complexity is with the notion of trajectory. Remember that, for him, time and therefore social mobility and occupational change are brought into the very definition of class. So those who are upwardly mobile might have more mixed or contradictory political stances, with aspects from their class of origin blended with aspects given by their current conditions, or they may have accrued a belief in self-responsibility or injustice on their way, depending on the class fraction from and to which they have travelled. Or we might have a whole section of the social space declining or rising with occupational change – certain jobs are disappearing or becoming less well-paid while others are becoming credentialized – and this will affect voting preferences as people look for ways to halt their decline or ensure their ascent. For example, Fenton (2012) has argued that the rightwards anti-immigration stance among certain sections of the working class dovetails with a declining trajectory in deindustrialized Britain, as they grope for a means of making sense of and battling against their fall and find parties offering explanations that appear to accord with practical experience – lack of jobs or social housing is due to there being more immigrants about (rather than neoliberal employment policy and the selling off of social housing). The point is that all of these complicating factors are part and parcel of class analysis for Bourdieu, but they are steamrollered by the measures of dealignment researchers and others who falsely assume that explicit 'class politics' exhaust what is of interest here, and only on this basis can they claim class and politics no longer go together.

Finally, to make sense of the apparent decline of talk of 'class' in politics and society we can turn to Bourdieu's concepts of 'class-making' and 'symbolic struggle': the constant wranglings and conflicts between those in the field of power over the legitimate way to characterize, conceptualize and describe the differences comprising the social space. From this perspective the decline of 'class' discourse, or more specifically of talk of 'class' in the political and media fields which frame so much of our daily experience, is in fact little more than the product of the dominance of the economic fraction of the dominant class in the field of power, as they can impose their vision of the world – individualism, since this most effectively reproduces and maintains their favoured capital via a programme of low taxes, small state etc. – as the legitimate one. In the UK this came in a particularly petite bourgeoisie authoritarian flavour on account of Margaret Thatcher's own class of origin, and her statements on class recounted earlier can be seen in this light.

This has obvious consequences for understanding the shifting nature of identities. To reiterate, Bourdieu distinguishes between classes 'on paper' – the actual clusters of people in social space on the basis of their capital – and classes in discourse – the various interpretations and representations of these clusters amongst people which may or may not involve the explicit term 'class'. A person's social identity is not *only* their explicit identification with specific groups or labels, therefore, but more fundamentally their implicit sense of their social position in relation to others, their sense of being above or below people, of being near or far from them socially, on the basis of a perception of the other's and their own place in social space. This is, of course, given by the clothes they wear, the sports they play, the leisure activities they engage in, the way they behave and so on – the symbols in symbolic space produced by dispositions of class, in other words. So identity is about whether we feel we fit in somewhere (a university, certain neighbourhoods, workplaces, sporting events, shops), or among certain people, whether we feel like a fish out of water and whether we feel superior or inferior, shame or disgust, if that is the case.

Now this can and does often draw on the discourse of 'classes': people do actually still use the labels of 'class' happily and spontaneously, with all the associated characteristics (work, education, behaviour, morals), to place themselves in relation to others (Atkinson, 2010). This may be, as Mike Savage (2000) argued, to make a case for being 'ordinary' in some way, not too high and not too low, or people might use it as an insult – 'chippie working-class oik', 'pretentious middle-class snob' or whatever – to mark their difference from others. But they may not draw on the discourse of 'class': they may use alternative labels instead to describe *exactly the same thing*, the same differences and divisions given by social space and symbolic space – 'posh', 'toffs', 'middle England/America', 'scum', 'hipster' and so on. The word 'chav' is a good example in England: this is a term applied in a very denigratory way (i.e. as symbolic violence) to those recognized via certain symbols – their clothes and behaviours – which correspond to a particular (low) position in the social space, yet people who use it may not recognize it as a phenomenon of 'class', might even explicitly claim it has nothing to do with it and would refuse to sign themselves up to a class category in a survey (see Nayak, 2006; Jones, 2010).

Or, as Simon Charlesworth (2000) found in his ethnography of Rotherham, a northern English town hit hard by the disappearance of manufacturing, the dominated may lack *any* real meaningful discourse to articulate their angst and feelings of low self-worth compared to others at all, partly because of the rise of Thatcherism and individualism and partly because of a disappearance of the things that were considered key to 'class' in the popular mind: manufacturing, trade unions, close communities and the like. The dominated no longer have the symbols of strength and resistance traditionally associated with 'the working class', and instead feel not only worthless but nameless, and, precisely because of that, even more marginalized. Or it could be that the dominated acknowledge but reject class labels, as Beverley Skeggs (1997) found amongst a group of young women taking caring courses. They had the discourse available, they recognized it, but they distanced themselves from the idea of being 'working class', disassociated themselves from the term and preferred to be seen as classless, or if anything middle class, because the label 'working class', for these women, carried with it a stigma: it was to be seen as less respectable, less educated, violent and tasteless, because of the way it has been constituted in prevalent discourses perpetuated by the dominant through politics and the media (as 'benefits scroungers', 'irresponsible parents', 'shameless' and such like). So whereas critics of the concept of class might look at surveys and emphasize a lack of strong class identity, and therefore sure testament of its decline or insignificance, the Bourdieusian

class researcher actually investigating what people say themselves recognizes that identities remain hemmed in by a sense
of one's place and a desire for recognition, or *classed*, whatever actual labels are used.

Conclusion

To summarize: with the rise and solidification of capitalism
we had the emergence of 'class politics', with material struggles and conditions of life framed by the language of 'class',
but from the mid-twentieth century onwards, with growing
affluence, deindustrialization, neoliberal individualism and
globalization, new issues and conditions have emerged and
the argument has been that 'class' no longer provides a useful
or major framework for making sense of it. While that may
be true if one sticks to a Marxist or Weberian definition of
class, however, from a Bourdieusian point of view we can
recognize that while views, vocabularies and self-perceptions
may have changed they are still homologous with class positions. In this sense the message is the same as seen in previous
chapters: change in the specific substance of class differences
but persistence of its power to differentiate experience and,
therefore, who we are, what we believe and what we do.

Coda

Let me reiterate the two overriding arguments of the book. First of all, when it comes to theoretical debates within class research I think it is fair to say that Marxism has struggled to recover from the poststructuralist blow, for which it was partially responsible, that it received in the 1970s and 1980s. Marxism still, to be sure, thrives in certain circles: it remains fashionable in philosophical debates, or at least certain elements of it do; there are various heterodox Marxist 'schools' in geography and economics and so on; and it still attracts a lot of vague sympathy among those who do not actually study class directly. Within sociological class analysis, however, it is a fading force. Erik Olin Wright was the leading light, and even then only at the cost of dropping a lot of what Marx actually said. Yet even he is rather less research-active these days, and it seems he has trained up few, if any, protégés to take up, develop and apply his class scheme. This is not to say Marxism cannot and will not make a comeback – who can say? – but it is at a low ebb to say the least.

Notwithstanding the gaggle of smaller players jostling to be taken seriously, that leaves just two key perspectives battling it out: on the one hand, those allied or sympathetic to the Nuffield programme, and, on the other, those inspired by Bourdieu. The latter are on the rise, opening up new vistas, situating class at the centre of social and cultural theory once again and attracting growing numbers of researchers, particularly newer generations, and while this movement started out among qualitative researchers dissatisfied with quantitative approaches to class the fight has now spread to statistical research. Hence the Nuffield School, its dominance under threat, has gone on the defensive, attacking and challenging various aspects of Bourdieu's approach, or the work of those inspired by him, usually on the basis of partial or outdated interpretations. The sociologies of education and lifestyles have been particular battlegrounds thus far, but who knows where the struggle may erupt next.

I have clearly come down in favour of Bourdieu's approach, but even I can see there is still plenty of conceptual and empirical work to be done. In particular, further working-through and analysis of the relationship between class and gender, ethnicity and other social divisions is desirable – and it strikes me that while it may seem evident enough, simply describing other divisions as capitals or fields without a thorough exploration of how and why that is the case risks loosening the concepts and making them easier targets for critics to take apart. Two other areas in need of elaboration are domains in which Marxists have traditionally dominated: historical analysis and world-systems analysis. The first of these was hinted at in chapter 4, where a rewrite of historical development in terms of competing principles of recognition was suggested. The second takes in not only relations between nations within an overall global social space – which Abdelmalek Sayad (2004) and, more recently and comprehensively, Julian Go (2008) have broached – and the machinations of a global field of power – which Frédéric Lebaron (2008) has begun to open up – but also their effects on the major principles of recognition, difference and struggle within nation states. Economic and cultural capital are not universal forms of symbolic value, but they are increasingly implicated in the rise of 'new middle classes' in developing and/or post-socialist nations such as India, China and Russia where, historically, other forms of capital (the political capital of party connections, for instance) have tended to dominate. An analysis of the structure of political and economic oppositions and the strategies they engender – not least in terms of weakening borders, deepened trade relations and thus the unequal circulation of goods, ideas and people – will give clues to the social genesis of the transformations of the social fabric felt and experienced by individuals from Beijing to Bangalore.

But then again, sociology is a field like any other within the field of power, with its internal struggles and strategies, its own dominant and dominated and its own conservatives and revolutionaries. Bourdieu may be coming to prominence now, not only in class research but across multiple 'special-isms', and further conceptual, historical and empirical work may further that advance. But there is nothing to rule out the possibility that Bourdieusian research will itself be overturned by some new upstart perspective before too long – such is, ironically, the nature of intellectual development. We can only hope that scientific principles outweigh political ones in the process and that any new vision of the social world, and the place of class within it, offers a better approximation of how things are.

The second message of the book, the more substantive one, is that, despite all the changes of the last fifty, or even a hundred, years, class has not gone away. That is because class is a *relative*, or better yet *relational*, concept: even if everyone went to university, or lived to be over a hundred, or became more liberal, there would still be some difference, and thus some site of denigration and conflict, within those new trends on the basis of resources possessed – types of universities, quality of life, degree of liberalism and so on. Those who criticize class are those who focus on absolute differences alone, or on the particular substance of class at some time point (jobs, education levels, health and so on), seeing them as solely constitutive or demonstrative of class, and those who confuse the labels we use to describe the world with the nature of the world itself. Bourdieu's theory is by no means alone in focusing on relative differences, but it does throw them into especially sharp relief since, in his view, as long as there is difference there will be class. Indeed, as he himself once put it, to deny the existence of classes is, in the last analysis, to deny the existence of difference (Bourdieu, 1998) – something which, so long as we quest for recognition at the expense of one another, is unlikely to disappear any time soon.

This raises the question famously posed by Lenin a hundred years ago: what is to be done? Since even Marxists admit we cannot rely on the dominated suddenly rising up and abolishing inequality, and since class differences are rooted in the most human search for justification and purpose in life, what can actually be done to make the world a better place? Perhaps the only thing that can be done – and this was certainly Bourdieu's view in his later years – is to raise awareness as widely as possible, in whatever way we can, that the problems, worries, suffering, stresses and pains in people's lives are not inevitable or freely chosen but are produced by the way society is set up, and that 'what society has done, it can, armed with this knowledge, undo' (Bourdieu, 1999c: 629). This is an injunction to those of us in the intellectual game, of course, but also to other readers of this text – students in particular – who will enter jobs or worlds where they might have some capacity to be able to speak out to and for others.

References

Abercrombie, N. and Urry, J. (1983) *Capital, Labour and the Middle Classes*. London: Allen and Unwin.

Acker, J. (1973) 'Women and Social Stratification: A Case of Intellectual Sexism' *American Journal of Sociology*, 78(4): 936–45.

Adkins, L. and Skeggs, B. (Eds.) (2004) *Feminism After Bourdieu*. Oxford: Blackwell.

Ahrne, G. (1991) 'Class and Society' in J. Clark, C. Modgil and S. Modgil (Eds.) *John H. Goldthorpe: Consensus and Controversy*. London: Falmer Press, pp. 65–73.

Althusser, L. (1971) *Lenin and Philosophy and Other Essays*. New York: Monthly Review Press.

Anthias, F. (2001) 'The Concept of Social Division and Theorising Stratification' *Sociology*, 35(4): 835–54.

Apple, M. (1978) *Ideology and Curriculum*. London: Routledge and Kegan Paul.

Apple, M. (1982) *Education and Power*. London: Routledge and Kegan Paul.

Archer, L., Hutchings, N. and Ross, A. (2003) *Higher Education and Social Class*. London: RoutledgeFalmer.

Archer, M. (2007) *Making Our Way Through the World*. Cambridge: Cambridge University Press.

Archer, M. (2013) *The Reflexive Imperative in Late Modernity*. Cambridge: Cambridge University Press.

Atkinson, W. (2009) 'Rethinking the Work–Class Nexus: Theoretical Foundations for Recent Trends' *Sociology*, 43(5): 896–912.

Atkinson, W. (2010) *Class, Individualization and Late Modernity: In Search of the Reflexive Worker*. Basingstoke: Palgrave Macmillan.

Atkinson, W. (2011a) 'The Context and Genesis of Musical Tastes: Omnivorousness Debunked, Bourdieu Buttressed' *Poetics*, 39(3): 169–86.

Atkinson, W. (2011b) 'From Sociological Fictions to Social Fictions: Some Bourdieusian Reflections on the Concepts of "Institutional Habitus" and "Family Habitus"' *British Journal of Sociology of Education*, 32(3): 331–47.

Atkinson, W. (2012a) '*Reproduction* Revisited' *Sociological Review*, 60(4): 734–52.

Atkinson, W. (2012b) 'Economic Crisis and Classed Everyday Life' in W. Atkinson, S. Roberts and M. Savage (Eds.) *Class Inequality in Austerity Britain*. Basingstoke: Palgrave Macmillan, pp. 13–32.

Atkinson, W. (2014) 'A Sketch of "Family" as a Field: From Realised Category to Space of Struggle' *Acta Sociologica*, 57(3): 223–35.

Atkinson, W. and Bradley, H. (2013) *Ordinary Lives in Contemporary Britain*. SPAIS Working Paper No. 8–13, University of Bristol. Available at: http://www.bristol.ac.uk/spais/research/workingpapers.

Atkinson, W. and Deeming, C. (forthcoming) 'Class and Cuisine in Contemporary Britain: The Social Space, the Space of Food and Their Homology' *Sociological Review*.

Atkinson, W. and Rosenlund, L. (2014) *Mapping the British Social Space: Toward a Bourdieusian Class Scheme*. SPAIS Working Paper No. 2–14, University of Bristol. Available at: http://www.bristol.ac.uk/spais/research/workingpapers.

Atkinson, W., Roberts, S. and Savage, M. (2012) 'Introduction: A Critical Sociology of the Age of Austerity' in W. Atkinson, S. Roberts and M. Savage (Eds.) *Class Inequality in Austerity Britain: Power, Difference and Suffering*. Basingstoke: Palgrave Macmillan, pp. 1–12.

Balibar, E. and Wallerstein, I. (1991) *Race, Nation, Class*. London: Verso.

Ball, S. (2003) *Class Strategies and the Education Market*. London: RoutledgeFalmer.

Barrett, M. (1980) *Women's Oppression Today*. London: Verso.

Barrett, M. (1991) *The Politics of Truth*. Cambridge: Polity.

Bartley, M. (2004) *Health Inequality*. Cambridge: Polity.

Bauman, Z. (2001) *The Individualized Society*. Cambridge: Polity.

Beck, U. (1992) *Risk Society*. London: Sage.

Beck, U. (2000) *What is Globalization?* Cambridge: Polity.

Becker, G. (1978) *The Economic Approach to Human Behavior*. Chicago: University of Chicago Press.

Bell, D. (1973) *The Coming of Post-Industrial Society*. New York: Basic Books.

Bell, D. (1979) *The Cultural Contradictions of Capitalism* (2nd edn). London: Heinemann.

Bennett, T., Savage, M., Silva, E., Gayo-Cal, M. and Wright, D. (2009) *Culture, Class, Distinction*. London: Routledge.

Bernstein, B. (1971) *Class, Codes and Control*. London: Paladin.

Blanden, J., Gregg, P. and Machin, S. (2005) *Intergenerational Mobility in Europe and North America*. London: Centre for Economic Performance and Sutton Trust.

Blanden, J., Gregg, P. and Macmillan, L. (2013) 'Intergenerational Persistence in Income and Social Class: The Effect of Within-Group Inequality' *Journal of the Royal Statistical Society*, Series A, 176(2): 1–23.

Blau, P. and Duncan, O. D. (1967) *The American Occupational Structure*. New York: John Wiley and Sons.

Blaxter, M. (1992) *Health and Lifestyles*. London: Routledge.

Boltanski, L. (1987) *The Making of a Class*. Cambridge: Cambridge University Press.

Bond, R. and Saunders, P. (1999) 'Routes of Success: Influences on the Occupational Attainment of Young British Males' *British Journal of Sociology*, 50(2): 217–49.

Bott, E. (1971) *Family and Social Network* (2nd edn). London: Tavistock.

Bottero, W. (2005) *Stratification*. London: Routledge.

Boudon, R. (1974) *Education, Opportunity and Social Inequality*. New York: John Wiley and Sons.

Bourdieu, P. (1980) 'A Diagram of Social Position and Lifestyle' *Media, Culture and Society*, 2(3): 255–9.

Bourdieu, P. (1984) *Distinction*. London: Routledge.

Bourdieu, P. (1987) 'What Makes a Social Class?' *Berkeley Journal of Sociology*, 32: 1–17.

Bourdieu, P. (1988) *Homo Academicus*. Cambridge: Polity.

Bourdieu, P. (1990a) *In Other Words*. Cambridge: Polity.

Bourdieu, P. (1990b) *The Logic of Practice*. Cambridge: Polity.

Bourdieu, P. (1991) *Language and Symbolic Power*. Cambridge: Polity.

Bourdieu, P. (1993) *Sociology in Question*. London: Sage.

Bourdieu, P. (1996) *The State Nobility*. Cambridge: Polity.

Bourdieu, P. (1998) *Practical Reason*. Cambridge: Polity.

Bourdieu, P. (1999a) 'Site Effects' in P. Bourdieu et al., *The Weight of the World*. Cambridge: Polity, pp. 123–9.

Bourdieu, P. (1999b) 'The Contradictions of Inheritance' in P. Bourdieu et al., *The Weight of the World*. Cambridge: Polity, pp. 507–13.

Bourdieu, P. (1999c) 'Postscript' in P. Bourdieu et al., *The Weight of the World*. Cambridge: Polity, pp. 627–9.

Bourdieu, P. (2000) *Pascalian Meditations*. Cambridge: Polity.

Bourdieu, P. (2001) *Masculine Domination*. Cambridge: Polity.

Bourdieu, P. (2004a) 'From the King's House to the Reason of State' *Constellations*, 11(1): 16–36.

Bourdieu, P. (2004b) *Science of Science and Reflexivity*. Cambridge: Polity.

Bourdieu, P. (2008) *The Bachelors' Ball*. Cambridge: Polity.

Bourdieu, P. (2014) *On the State*. Cambridge: Polity.

Bourdieu, P. and Passeron, J.-C. (1977/1990) *Reproduction in Society, Education and Culture*. London: Sage.

Bourdieu, P. and Passeron, J.-C. (1979) *The Inheritors*. Chicago: University of Chicago Press.

Bourgois, P. (2003) *In Search of Respect*. Cambridge: Cambridge University Press.

Bowles, S. and Gintis, H. (1976) *Schooling in Capitalist America*. New York: Basic Books.

Braverman, H. (1974) *Labor and Monopoly Capital*. New York: Monthly Review Press.

Breen, R. (Ed.) (2004) *Social Mobility in Europe*. Oxford: Oxford University Press.

Breen, R. and Goldthorpe, J. (1999) 'Class Inequality and Meritocracy' *British Journal of Sociology*, 50(1): 1–27.

Breen, R. and Goldthorpe, J. (2002) 'Merit, Mobility and Method' *British Journal of Sociology*, 53(4): 575–82.

Brubaker, R. (2004) *Ethnicity Without Groups*. Cambridge, MA: Harvard University Press.

Bukodi, E. and Goldthorpe, J. (2013) 'Decomposing "Social Origins": The Effects of Parents' Class, Status and Education on the Educational Attainment of Their Children' *European Sociological Review*, 26(5): 1024–39.

Butler, J. (1990) *Gender Trouble*. London: Routledge.

Calhoun, C. (1993) 'Habitus, Field and Capital: The Question of Historical Specificity' in C. Calhoun, E. LiPuma and M. Postone (Eds.) *Bourdieu: Critical Perspectives*. Cambridge: Polity, pp. 61–88.

Calhoun, C. (1994) *Social Theory and the Politics of Identity*. Oxford: Blackwell.

Callinicos, A. (1993) *Race and Class*. London: Bookmarks.

Calvert, P. (1982) *The Concept of Class*. London: Hutchinson.

Cannadine, D. (1998) *Class*. London: Penguin.

Carchedi, G. (1977) *On the Economic Identification of Social Classes*. London: Routledge and Kegan Paul.

CCCS (1982) *The Empire Strikes Back*. London: Hutchinson.

Chan, T. W. and Goldthorpe, J. H. (2010) 'Social Status and Cultural Consumption' in T. W. Chan (Ed.) *Social Status and Cultural Consumption*. Cambridge: Cambridge University Press, pp. 1–27.

Charlesworth, S. (2000) *A Phenomenology of Working Class Experience*. Cambridge: Cambridge University Press.

Clark, T. and Lipset, S. M. (Eds.) (2001) *The Breakdown of Class Politics*. Baltimore: Johns Hopkins University Press.

Cockerham, W. (2013) *Social Causes of Health and Disease*. Cambridge: Polity.

Coleman, J. (1986) 'Social Theory, Social Research, and a Theory of Action' *American Journal of Sociology*, 91(6): 1309–35.

Coleman, J., Campbell, E., Hobson, C., McPartland, J., Mood, A., Weinfeld, F. and York, R. (1966) *Equality of Educational Opportunity*. Washington, DC: US Government Printing Office.

Coles, T. (2007) 'Negotiating the Field of Masculinity' *Men and Masculinities*, 12(1): 30–44.

Collins, P. H. (2001) *Black Feminist Thought*. London: Routledge.

Collins, R. (1979) *The Credential Society*. London: Routledge and Kegan Paul.

Connell, R. (1983) *Which Way is Up?* London: Allen and Unwin.

Connell, R. (2005) *Masculinities*. Cambridge: Polity.

Cox, O. C. (1948) *Caste, Class and Race*. New York: Doubleday.

Crompton, R. (2008) *Class and Stratification*. Cambridge: Polity.

Crompton, R. and Scott, J. (2005) 'Class Analysis: Beyond the Cultural Turn' in F. Devine, M. Savage, J. Scott and R. Crompton (Eds.) *Rethinking Class*. Basingstoke: Palgrave Macmillan, pp. 186–203.

Crook, S., Pakulski, J. and Waters, M. (1992) *Postmodernization*. London: Sage.

Crow, G. and Allen, G. (1994) *Community Life*. Hemel Hempstead: Harvester Wheatsheaf.

Dahrendorf, R. (1959) *Class and Class Conflict in Industrial Society*. London: Routledge and Kegan Paul.

Davis, K. and Moore, W. (1945) 'Some Principles of Stratification' *American Sociological Review*, 10(2): 242–9.

Delphy, C. (1984) *Close to Home: A Materialist Analysis of Women's Oppression*. London: Hutchinson.

Dennis, N., Henriques, F. and Slaughter, C. (1969) *Coal is Our Life: An Analysis of a Yorkshire Mining Community* (2nd edn). London: Tavistock.

Devine, F. (1998) 'Class Analysis and the Stability of Class Relations' *Sociology*, 32(1): 23–42.

Devine, F. (2004) *Class Practices*. Cambridge: Cambridge University Press.

Dolby, N. and Dimitriadis, G. (Eds.) (2004) *Learning to Labor in New Times*. London: Routledge.

Dorling, D. (2013) *Unequal Health: The Scandal of Our Times*. Bristol: Policy Press.

Dubois, V., Méon, J.-M. and Pierru, E. (2013) *The Sociology of Wind Bands*. Farnham: Ashgate.

Eder, K. (1993) *The New Politics of Class*. London: Sage.

Elias, N. (2000) *The Civilizing Process*. Cambridge: Blackwell.

Elias, N. and Scotson, J. (1990) *The Established and the Outsiders*. London: Sage.

Engels, F. (1845/1987) *The Condition of the Working Class in England*. London: Penguin.

Engels, F. (1990) *The Origins of Private Property, Family and the State*. London: Penguin.

Erikson, R. (1984) 'Social Class of Men, Women and Families' *Sociology*, 18(4): 500–14.

Erikson, R. and Goldthorpe, J. (1992) *The Constant Flux*. Oxford: Clarendon Press.

Erikson, R. and Goldthorpe, J. (2010) 'Has Social Mobility in Britain Decreased?' *British Journal of Sociology*, 61(2): 211–30.

Esping-Anderson, G. (Ed.) (1993) *Changing Classes*. London: Sage.

Eurostat (2013) *European Social Statistics*. Luxembourg: European Union.

Evans, G. (1993) 'The Decline of Class Divisions in Britain?' *British Journal of Sociology*, 44(3): 449–71.

Evans, G. (Ed.) (1999) *The End of Class Politics?* Oxford: Oxford University Press.

Evans, G. and Tilley, J. (2012) 'How Parties Shape Class Politics' *British Journal of Political Science*, 42(1): 137–61.

Featherman, D., Jones, F. and Hauser, R. (1975) 'Assumptions of Social Mobility Research in the US' *Social Science Research*, 4: 329–60.

Featherstone, M. (1991) *Consumer Culture and Postmodernism*. London: Sage.

Feinstein, L. (2003) 'Inequality in the Early Cognitive Development of British Children in the 1970 Cohort' *Economica*, 70(277): 73–97.

Fenton, S. (2012) 'Resentment, Class and Social Sentiment about the Nation' *Ethnicities*, 12(4): 465–83.

Firestone, S. (1970) *The Dialectic of Sex*. New York: Morrow.

Flemmen, M. (2013) 'Putting Bourdieu to Work for Class Analysis' *British Journal of Sociology*, 64(2): 325–43.

France, A., Bottrell, D. and Haddon, E. (2012) 'Managing Everyday Life' *Journal of Youth Studies*, 16(5): 597–611.

Freire, P. (1970) *The Pedagogy of the Oppressed*. London: Continuum.

Friedman, S. (2012) 'Cultural Omnivores or Culturally Homeless?' *Poetics*, 40(5): 467–89.

Friedman, S. (2014) 'The Price of the Ticket: Rethinking the Experience of Social Mobility' *Sociology*, 48(2): 352–68.

Friedman, S. (2015) 'Habitus Clivé and the Emotional Imprint of Social Mobility' *Sociological Review*.

Galbraith, J. K. (1992) *The Culture of Contentment*. London: Penguin.

Gallie, D. (2000) 'The Labour Force' in H. Halsey and J. Webb (Eds.) *Twentieth-Century British Social Trends*. Basingstoke: Macmillan, pp. 281–323.

Gardiner, J. (1977) 'Women in the Labour Process and Class Structure' in A. Hunt (Ed.) *Class and Class Structure*. London: Lawrence and Wishart, pp. 155–64.

Gartman, D. (1991) 'Culture as Class Symbolization or Mass Reification?' *American Journal of Sociology*, 97(2): 421–47.

Gerteis, J. and Savage, M. (1998) 'The Salience of Class in Britain and America' *British Journal of Sociology*, 49(2): 252–74.

Giddens, A. (1981) *The Class Structure of the Advanced Societies* (2nd edn). London: Hutchinson.

Giddens, A. (1991) *Modernity and Self-Identity*. Cambridge: Polity.

Gilroy, P. (1987/2002) *There Ain't No Black in the Union Jack* (2nd edn). London: Routledge.

Glaesser, J. and Cooper, B. (2014) 'Using Rational Action Theory and Bourdieu's Habitus Theory Together to Account for Educational Decision-Making in England and Germany' *Sociology*, 48(3): 463–81.

Glass, D. (Ed.) (1954) *Social Mobility in Britain*. London: Routledge and Kegan Paul.

Go, J. (2008) 'Global Fields and Imperial Forms' *Sociological Theory*, 26(3): 201–29.

Goldberg, D. T. (1987) 'Raking the Field of the Discourse of Racism' *Journal of Black Studies*, 18(1): 58–71.

Goldthorpe, J. (1980) *Social Mobility and Class Structure in Modern Britain*. Oxford: Clarendon Press.

Goldthorpe, J. (1982) 'On the Service Class, its Formation and Future' in A. Giddens and G. Mckenzie (Eds.) *Social Class and the Division of Labour*. Cambridge: Cambridge University Press, pp. 162–85.

Goldthorpe, J. (1983) 'Women and Class Analysis: In Defence of the Conventional View' *Sociology*, 17(4): 465–88.

Goldthorpe, J. (1987) *Social Mobility and Class Structure in Modern Britain* (2nd edn). Oxford: Clarendon Press.

Goldthorpe, J. (1995) 'The Service Class Revisited' in M. Savage and T. Butler (Eds.) *Social Change and the Middle Classes*. London: UCL Press, pp. 313–29.

Goldthorpe, J. (1999) 'Modelling the Pattern of Class Voting in British Elections, 1964–1992' in G. Evans (Ed.) *The End of Class Politics?* Oxford: Oxford University Press, pp. 59–82.

Goldthorpe, J. (2007a) *On Sociology* (2 vols.). Oxford: Oxford University Press.

Goldthorpe, J. (2007b) 'Cultural Capital: Some Critical Observations' in S. Scherer, R. Pollak, G. Otte and M. Gangl (Eds.) *From Origin to Destination*. Chicago: University of Chicago Press, pp. 78–101.

Goldthorpe, J. (2010) 'Analysing Social Inequality: A Critique of Two Recent Contributions from Economics and Epidemiology' *European Sociological Review*, 26(6): 731–44.

Goldthorpe, J. (2013) 'Understanding – and Misunderstanding – Social Mobility in Britain' *Journal of Social Policy*, 42(3): 431–50.

Goldthorpe, J. and Jackson, M. (2007) 'Intergenerational Class Mobility in Contemporary Britain' *British Journal of Sociology*, 58(4): 525–46.

Goldthorpe, J. and Marshall, G. (1992) 'The Promising Future of Class Analysis' *Sociology*, 26(3): 381–400.

Gorz, A. (1982) *Farewell to the Working Class*. London: Pluto Press.

Graham, H. (2007) *Unequal Lives*. Milton Keynes: Open University Press.

Gramsci, A. (1973) *Selections from the Prison Notebooks*. London: Lawrence and Wishart.

Green, A. I. (Ed.) (2014) *Sexual Fields*. Chicago: University of Chicago Press.

Grusky, D. (2005) 'Foundations of a Neo-Durkheimian Class Analysis' in E. O. Wright (Ed.) *Approaches to Class Analysis*. Cambridge: Cambridge University Press, pp. 51–81.

Gubbay, J. (1997) 'A Marxist Critique of Weberian Class Analyses' *Sociology*, 31(1): 73–89.

Güveli, A., Need, A. and De Graaf, N. (2007) 'The Rise of "New" Social Classes within the Service Class in The Netherlands' *Acta Sociologica*, 50(2): 129–46.

Habermas, J. (1981) 'New Social Movements' *Telos*, 49: 33–7.

Habermas, J. (1987) *The Theory of Communicative Action* (2 vols.). Cambridge: Polity.

Hage, G. (2000) *White Nation*. New York: Routledge.

Hakim, C. (2012) *Honey Money*. London: Penguin.

Hall, S. (1980) 'Race, Articulation and Societies Structured in Dominance' in UNESCO (Ed.) *Sociological Theories: Race and Colonialism*. Paris: UNESCO, pp. 305–45.

Hall, S. and Jefferson, T. (1975/2006) *Resistance through Rituals*. London: Routledge.

Halsey, A. H., Heath, A. F. and Ridge, J. M. (1980) *Origins and Destinations*. Oxford: Clarendon Press.

Harrits, G., Prieur, A., Rosenlund, L. and Skjott-Larsen, J. (2010) 'Class and Politics in Denmark: Are Both Old and New Politics Structured by Class?' *Scandinavian Political Studies*, 33(1): 1–27.

Hartmann, H. (1979) 'The Unhappy Marriage of Marxism and Feminism' *Capital & Class*, 3(2): 1–33.

Heath, A. and Britten, N. (1984) 'Women's Jobs Do Make a Difference' *Sociology*, 18(4): 475–90.

Heath, A., Jowell, R. and Curtice, J. (1985) *How Britain Votes*. Oxford: Pergamon Press.

Heath, A., Curtice, J. and Elgenius, G. (2010) 'Individualization and the Decline of Class Identity' in M. Wetherell (Ed.) *Identity in the 21st Century*. Basingstoke: Palgrave Macmillan, pp. 21–40.

Hedström, P. (2005) *Dissecting the Social*. Cambridge: Cambridge University Press.

Herrnstein, R. and Murray, C. (1994) *The Bell Curve*. New York: Free Press.

Hobsbawm, E. (2007) 'Critical Sociology and Social History' *Sociological Research Online*, 12(4): http://www.socresonline.org.uk/12/4/2.html.

Hoggart, R. (1957) *The Uses of Literacy*. Harmondsworth: Penguin.

Holt, D. (1997) 'Distinction in America? Recovering Bourdieu's Theory of Tastes from its Critics' *Poetics*, 25: 93–120.

Honneth, A. (1995) *The Struggle for Recognition*. Cambridge: Polity.

Houtman, D. (2003) *Class and Politics in Contemporary Social Science*. New York: Aldine de Gruyter.

Huppatz, K. (2012) *Gender Capital at Work*. London: Palgrave Macmillan.

Inglehart, R. (1977) *The Silent Revolution*. Princeton: Princeton University Press.

Jackson, B. and Marsden, D. (1962) *Education and the Working Class*. London: Routledge and Kegan Paul.

Jackson, M., Erikson, R., Goldthorpe, J. and Yaish, M. (2007) 'Primary and Secondary Effects in Class Differentials in Educational Attainment' *Acta Sociologica*, 50(3): 211–29.

Jenkins, R. (1983) *Lads, Citizens and Ordinary Kids*. London: Routledge and Kegan Paul.

Jenkins, R. (2002) *Pierre Bourdieu*. London: Routledge.

Johnson, T. (1991) 'Ideology and Action in the Work of Goldthorpe' in J. Clark, C. Modgil and S. Modgil (Eds.) *John H. Goldthorpe: Consensus and Controversy*. London: Falmer Press, pp. 373–91.

Jones, O. (2010) *Chav*. London: Verso.

Kerr, C., Dunlop, J., Harbison, F. and Myers, C. (1960) *Industrialism and Industrial Man*. Cambridge, MA: Harvard University Press.

Laclau, E. and Mouffe, C. (1985) *Hegemony and Socialist Strategy*. London: Verso.

Lahire, B. (2011) *The Plural Actor*. Cambridge: Polity.

Lareau, A. (2003) *Unequal Childhoods*. Berkeley: University of California Press.

Lash, S. (1990) *Sociology of Postmodernism*. London: Sage.

Lash, S. and Urry, J. (1994) *Economies of Signs and Space*. London: Sage.

Lawler, S. (2000) *Mothering the Self*. London: Routledge.

Lebaron, F. (2008) 'Central Bankers in the Contemporary Global Field of Power' in M. Savage and K. Williams (Eds.) *Remembering Elites*. Oxford: Blackwell, pp. 121–44.

Lee, M. A. and Mather, M. (2008) 'US Labour Force Trends' *Population Bulletin*, 63(2). Available at: http://www.prb.org/pdf08/63.2uslabor.pdf.

Lenski, G. (1954) 'Status Crystallization: A Non-Vertical Dimension of Social Status' *American Sociological Review*, 19(4): 405–13.

Lipset, S. M. (1960) *Political Man*. London: Heinemann.

Lipset, S. M. and Bendix, R. (1959) *Social Mobility in Industrial Society*. Berkeley: University of California Press.

Lipset, S. M. and Rokkan, S. (Eds.) (1967) *Party Systems and Voter Alignments*. New York: Free Press.

Lockwood, D. (1958) *The Blackcoated Worker*. London: Allen and Unwin.

Lockwood, D. (1966) 'Sources of Variation in Working-Class Images of Society' *Sociological Review*, 14(3): 249–67.

Lovell, T. (2000) 'Thinking Feminism With and Against Bourdieu' *Feminist Theory*, 1(1): 11–32.

Lukács, G. (1971) *History and Class Consciousness*. London: Merlin.

Lynch, J., Smith, G. D., Kaplan, G. and House, J. (2000) 'Income Inequality and Mortality' *British Medical Journal*, 320: 1200–4.

Lynch, J., Smith, G. D., Hillemeier, M., Shaw, M., Raghunathan, T. and Kaplan, G. (2001) 'Income Inequality, the Psychosocial Environment, and Health' *Lancet*, 358: 194–200.

Lynch, J., Smith, G. D., Harper, S., Hillemeier, M., Ross, N., Kaplan, G. and Wolfson, M. (2004) 'Is Income Inequality a Determinant of Population Health?' *Milbank Quarterly*, 82(1): 5–99.

Lynd, R. and Lynd, H. (1929) *Middletown*. London: Constable.

Mac an Ghaill, M. (1994) *The Making of Men*. Buckingham: Open University Press.

Mahony, P. and Zmroczek, C. (Eds.) (1997) *Class Matters*. London: Taylor and Francis.

Mann, M. (1973) *Class Consciousness and Action Among the Western Working Class*. Basingstoke: Macmillan.

Mann, M. (1986) *The Sources of Social Power* (Vol. 1). Cambridge: Cambridge University Press.

Marcuse, H. (1964) *One-Dimensional Man*. London: Routledge and Kegan Paul.

Marmot, M. (2004) *Status Syndrome*. London: Bloomsbury.

Marshall, G. (1997) *Repositioning Class*. London: Sage.

Marshall, G., Rose, D., Newby, H. and Vogler, C. (1988) *Social Class in Modern Britain*. London: Routledge.

Marshall, G., Swift, A. and Roberts, S. (1997) *Against the Odds? Social Class and Social Justice in Industrial Societies*. Oxford: Clarendon Press.

Marx, K. (1844/1959) *Economic and Philosophical Manuscripts of 1844*. London: Lawrence and Wishart.

Marx, K. (1847/1955) *The Poverty of Philosophy*. London: Lawrence and Wishart.

Marx, K. (1852/1968) *The Eighteenth Brumaire of Louis Bonaparte* in *Selected Works*. London: Lawrence and Wishart, pp. 96–179.

Marx, K. (1859/1968) 'Preface to *A Contribution to a Critique of Political Economy*' in *Selected Works*. London: Lawrence and Wishart, pp. 180–4.

Marx, K. and Engels, F. (1845/1998) *The German Ideology*. New York: Prometheus.

Marx, K. and Engels, F. (1848/1998) *The Communist Manifesto*. Oxford: Oxford University Press.

McCall, L. (1992) 'Does Gender Fit?' *Theory and Society*, 21(6): 837–67.

McKenzie, L. (2012) 'The Stigmatised and De-Valued Working Class' in W. Atkinson, S. Roberts and M. Savage (Eds.) *Class Inequality in Austerity Britain*. Basingstoke: Palgrave Macmillan, pp. 128–44.

McRae, S. (1988) *Cross-Class Families*. Oxford: Oxford University Press.

McRobbie, A. (1991) *Feminism and Youth Culture*. London: Routledge.

Melucci, A. (1980) 'The New Social Movements: A Theoretical Approach' *Social Science Information*, 19(2): 199–226.

Miles, A., Savage, M. and Bühlmann, F. (2011) 'Telling a Modest Story: Accounts of Men's Upward Mobility from the National Child Development Study' *British Journal of Sociology*, 62(3): 418–41.

Miles, R. and Brown, M. (2003) *Racism* (2nd edn). London: Routledge.

Millett, K. (1971) *Sexual Politics*. London: Hart-Davis.

Modood, T. (2004) 'Capitals, Ethnic Identity and Educational Qualifications' *Cultural Trends*, 13(2): 87–105.

Modood, T., Berthoud, R., Lakey, J., Nazroo, J., Smith, P., Virdee, S. and Beishon, S. (1997) *Ethnic Minorities in Britain: Diversity and Disadvantage*. London: Policy Studies Institute.

Moi, T. (1991) 'Appropriating Bourdieu' *New Literary History*, 22(4): 1017–49.

Mommsen, W. (1977) 'Max Weber as a Critic of Marxism' *Canadian Journal of Sociology*, 2(4): 373–98.

Morris, L. and Scott, J. (1996) 'The Attenuation of Class Analysis' *British Journal of Sociology*, 47(1): 45–55.

Mottier, V. (2002) 'Masculine Domination' *Feminist Theory*, 3(3): 345–59.

Muntaner, C. and Lynch, J. (1999) 'Income Inequality, Social Cohesion and Class Relations' *International Journal of Health Services*, 29(1): 59–81.

Murphy, R. (1988) *Social Closure*. Oxford: Clarendon Press.

Navarro, V. (1976) *Medicine Under Capitalism*. London: Croom Helm.

Navarro, V. (1978) *Class Struggle, the State and Medicine*. London: Martin Robinson.

Navarro, V. (1986) *Crisis, Health and Medicine*. London: Tavistock.

Nayak, A. (2006) 'Displaced Masculinities: Chavs, Youth and Class in the Post-Industrial City' *Sociology*, 40(5): 813–31.

Offe, C. (1985) 'New Social Movements' *Social Research*, 52(4): 817–68.

ONS (Office for National Statistics) (2010) *Social Trends 40*. Basingstoke: Palgrave Macmillan.

ONS (Office for National Statistics) (2011) *Statistical Bulletin: Trends in Life Expectancy by the National Statistics Socio-Economic Classification 1982–2006*. Available at: http://www.ons.gov.uk/ons/taxonomy/index.html?nscl=Health+Inequalities.

ONS (Office for National Statistics) (2013) *Statistical Bulletin: Health Gaps by Socio-Economic Position of Occupations in England, Wales, English Regions and Local Authorities, 2011*.

Available at: http://www.ons.gov.uk/ons/taxonomy/index.html?n scl=Health+Inequalities.

Pakulski, J. and Waters, M. (1996) *The Death of Class*. London: Sage.

Parkin, F. (1979) *Marxism and Class Theory: A Bourgeois Critique*. London: Tavistock.

Parsons, T. (1954) *Essays in Sociological Theory*. New York: Free Press.

Passeron, J.-C. and Grignon, C. (1989) *Le Savant et le Populaire*. Paris: Seuil.

Peterson, R. A. (1992) 'Understanding Audience Segmentation: From Elite and Mass to Omnivore and Univore' *Poetics*, 21: 243–58.

Polanyi, K. (1957) *The Great Transformation*. Boston: Beacon Press.

Poulantzas, N. (1975) *Classes in Contemporary Capitalism*. London: Verso.

Prieur, A., Rosenlund, L. and Skjott-Larson, J. (2008) 'Cultural Capital Today: A Case Study from Denmark' *Poetics*, 36: 45–71.

Putnam, R. (2000) *Bowling Alone* (2nd edn). London: Simon and Schuster.

Reay, D. (1998) *Class Work*. London: UCL Press.

Reay, D., David, M. and Ball, S. (2005) *Degrees of Choice*. Stoke-on-Trent: Trentham Books.

Reay, D., Crozier, G. and James, D. (2011) *White Middle-Class Identities and Urban Schooling*. Basingstoke: Palgrave Macmillan.

Reich, M. (1981) *Racial Inequality*. Princeton: Princeton University Press.

Resnick, S. and Wolff, R. (2003) 'The Diversity of Class Analyses' *Critical Sociology*, 29(7): 7–27.

Rex, J. (1986) *Race and Ethnicity*. Buckingham: Open University Press.

Rex, J. and Tomlinson, S. (1979) *Colonial Immigrants in a British City: A Class Analysis*. London: Routledge and Kegan Paul.

Robinson, C. (1983) *Black Marxism*. London: Zed Books.

Robinson, W. I. (2004) *A Theory of Global Capitalism*. Baltimore: Johns Hopkins University Press.

Rose, D. and Harrison, E. (Eds.) (2011) *Social Class in Europe*. London: Routledge.

Rose, D. and Marshall, G. (1986) 'Constructing the (W)right Classes' *Sociology*, 20(3): 440–55.

Rose, D. and Pevalin, D. (Eds.) (2003) *A Researcher's Guide to the National Statistics Socio-Economic Classification*. London: Sage.

Rosenlund, L. (2009) *Exploring the City with Bourdieu*. Saarbrucken: VDM.

Said, E. (1978) *Orientalism*. London: Routledge.

Sarlvik, B. and Crewe, I. (1983) *Decade of Dealignment*. Cambridge: Cambridge University Press.

Sarup, M. (1979) *Marxism and Education*. London: Routledge and Kegan Paul.

Saunders, P. (1990) *Social Class and Stratification*. London: Routledge.

Saunders, P. (1995) 'Might Britain be a Meritocracy?' *Sociology*, 29(1): 23–41.

Saunders, P. (1997) 'Social Mobility in Britain' *Sociology*, 31(2): 261–88.

Saunders, P. (2002) 'A Reflection on the Meritocracy Debate' *British Journal of Sociology*, 53(4): 559–74.

Savage, M. (2000) *Class Analysis and Social Transformation*. Buckingham: Open University Press.

Savage, M. (2003) 'A New Class Paradigm?' *British Journal of Sociology of Education*, 24(4): 535–41.

Savage, M., Barlow, J., Dickens, P. and Fielding, T. (1992) *Property, Bureaucracy and Culture*. London: Routledge.

Savage, M. et al. (2013) 'A New Model of Social Class?' *Sociology*, 47(2): 219–50.

Sayad, A. (2004) *The Suffering of the Immigrant*. Cambridge: Polity.

Sayer, A. (2005) *The Moral Significance of Class*. Cambridge: Cambridge University Press.

Scambler, G. (2002) *Health and Social Change: A Critical Theory*. Buckingham: Open University Press.

Scott, J. (1991) *Who Rules Britain?* Cambridge: Polity.

Scott, J. (1996) *Stratification and Power*. Cambridge: Polity.

Seccombe, W. (1974) 'The Housewife and Her Labour Under Capitalism' *New Left Review*, 83: 3–24.

Sennett, R. and Cobb, J. (1977) *The Hidden Injuries of Class*. Cambridge: Cambridge University Press.

Shilling, C. (2003) *The Body and Social Theory*. London: Sage.

Skeggs, B. (1997) *Formations of Class and Gender*. London: Sage.

Skeggs, B. (2004) 'Context and Background: Pierre Bourdieu's Analysis of Class, Gender and Sexuality' in L. Adkins and B. Skeggs (Eds.) *Feminism After Bourdieu*. Oxford: Blackwell, pp. 19–33.

Skeggs, B. (2011) 'Imagining Personhood Differently' *Sociological Review*, 59(3): 498–513.

Skeggs, B. and Wood, H. (2011) *Reacting to Reality Television*. London: Routledge.

Sklair, L. (2001) *The Transnational Capitalist Class*. Oxford: Blackwell.

Stacey, M. (1960) *Tradition and Change: A Study of Banbury*. Oxford: Oxford University Press.

Stanworth, M. (1984) 'Women and Class Analysis' *Sociology*, 18(2): 159–70.

Steinmetz, G. (2007) *The Devil's Handwriting*. Chicago: University of Chicago Press.

Stewart, A., Prandy, L. and Blackburn, R. (1980) *Social Stratification and Occupations*. London: Macmillan.

Stubager, R. (2008) 'Education Effects on Authoritarian-Libertarian Values' *British Journal of Sociology*, 59(2): 327–50.

Tabar, P., Noble, G. and Poynting, S. (2010) *On Being Lebanese in Australia: Identity, Racism and the Ethnic Field*. Beirut: LAU Press.

Tomlinson, M. (1998) 'Changes in Tastes in Britain, 1985–1992' *British Food Journal*, 100(6): 295–301.

Torssander, J. and Erikson, R. (2010) 'Stratification and Mortality: A Comparison of Education, Class, Status and Income' *European Sociological Review*, 26(4): 465–74.

Townsend, P. and Davidson, N. (1982) 'The Black Report' in *Inequalities in Health: The Black Report and the Health Divide*. London: Penguin, pp. 31–213.

Treiman, D. (1977) *Occupational Prestige in Comparative Perspective*. New York: Academic Press.

Van de Werfhorst, H. and de Graaf, N. (2004) 'The Sources of Political Orientations in Post-Industrial Society' *British Journal of Sociology*, 55(2): 211–35.

Van Eijk, C. (1999) 'Socialisation, Education and Lifestyle' *Poetics*, 26: 309–28.

Vandebroeck, D. (2013) *Harnessing the Flesh: Social Class and Reflexive Embodiment*. Unpublished PhD thesis, Free University of Brussels, Belgium.

Veenstra, G. (2007) 'Social Space, Social Class, and Bourdieu' *Health and Place*, 13: 14–31.

Vincent, C. and Ball, S. (2007) 'Making Up the Middle-Class Child' *Sociology*, 41(6): 1061–77.

Virdee, S. (2014) *Racism, Class and the Racialized Outsider*. Basingstoke: Palgrave Macmillan.

Wacquant, L. (1995) 'Pugs at Work: Bodily Capital and Bodily Labour Among Professional Boxers' *Body and Society*, 1(1): 65–93.

Wacquant, L. (1999) 'Inside "the Zone"' in P. Bourdieu et al., *The Weight of the World*. Cambridge: Polity, pp. 140–67.

Wacquant, L. (2004) *Body and Soul*. Oxford: Oxford University Press.

Wacquant, L. (2009) *Punishing the Poor*. Cambridge: Polity.

Waitzkin, H. (1983) *The Second Sickness*. New York: Free Press.

Wakeling, P. (2005) 'La noblesse d'état anglaise? Social Class and Progression to Postgraduate Study' *British Journal of Sociology of Education*, 26(4): 505–22.

Walkerdine, V. and Lucey, H. (1989) *Democracy in the Kitchen*. London: Virago.

Walkerdine, V., Lucey, H. and Melody, J. (2001) *Growing Up Girl*. Basingstoke: Palgrave Macmillan.

Weber, M. (1978) *Economy and Society* (2 vols.). Berkeley: University of California Press

Weber, M. (1905/2001) *The Protestant Ethic and the Spirit of Capitalism*. London: Routledge.

Wilkinson, R. and Pickett, K. (2009) *The Spirit Level*. London: Penguin.

Williams, R. (2001) *Keywords* (new edn). London: Fontana.

Williams, S. (1995) 'Theorising Class, Health and Lifestyles: Can Bourdieu Help Us?' *Sociology of Health and Illness*, 17(5): 577–604.

Willis, P. (1977) *Learning to Labour*. Farnborough: Saxon House.

Wills, W., Backett-Milburn, K., Roberts, M.-L. and Lawton, J. (2011) 'The Framing of Social Class Distinctions Through Family Food and Eating Practices' *Sociological Review*, 59(4): 725–40.

Wilson, W. J. (1980) *The Declining Significance of Race* (2nd edn). Chicago: University of Chicago Press.

Wright, E. O. (1978) *Class, Crisis and the State*. London: Verso.

Wright, E. O. (1979) *Class Structure and Income Determination*. New York: Academic Press.

Wright, E. O. (1985) *Classes*. London: Verso.

Wright, E. O. (1996) 'The Continuing Relevance of Class Analysis' *Theory and Society*, 25(5): 693–716.

Wright, E. O. (1997) *Class Counts*. Cambridge: Cambridge University Press.

Wright, E. O. (2002) 'The Shadow of Exploitation in Weber's Class Analysis' *American Sociological Review*, 67(6): 832–53.

Wright, E. O. (2005) 'Foundations of a Neo-Marxist Class Analysis' in E. O. Wright (Ed.) *Approaches to Class Analysis*. Cambridge: Cambridge University Press, pp. 4–30.

Wright, E. O. (2009) 'Understanding Class' *New Left Review*, 60: 101–16.

Wright, E. O. (2010) *Envisioning Real Utopias*. London: Verso.

Wright, E. O. and Martin, B. (1987) 'The Transformation of the American Class Structure, 1960–1980' *American Journal of Sociology*, 93(1): 1–29.

Wright, E. O. and Singlemann, J. (1982) 'Proletarianization in the Changing American Class Structure' *American Journal of Sociology*, 88(supplement): 176–209.

Wright, E. O. et al. (1989) *The Debate on Classes*. London: Verso.

Wright, E. O., Levine, A. and Sober, E. (1992) *Reconstructing Marxism*. London: Verso.

Young, M. and Willmott, P. (1962) *Family and Kinship in East London*. Harmondsworth: Penguin.

Young, R. (1990) *White Mythologies*. London: Routledge.

Index